ISLE OF MAN

...lks

CW01045463

**25 GLEN WALKS INCLUDING
ALL MANX NATIONAL GLENS
ALAN COOPER**

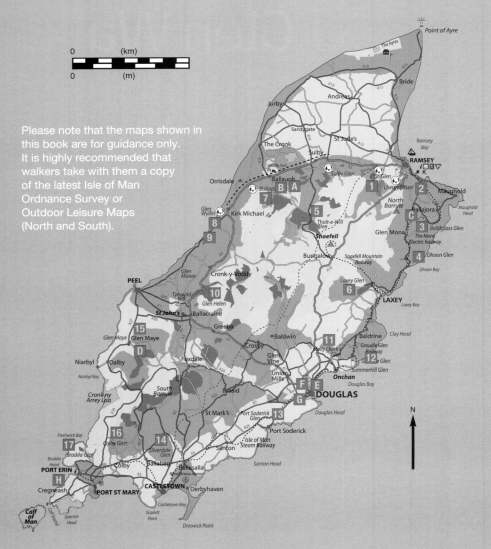

Please note that the maps shown in this book are for guidance only. It is highly recommended that walkers take with them a copy of the latest Isle of Man Ordnance Survey or Outdoor Leisure Maps (North and South).

ISBN No. 978-1-911177-82-1

Index of Walks

Ref.	Name	Terrain	OS map ref.
	MANX NATIONAL GLEN WALKS		
1	Elfin Glen / Lhergy Frissel	Moderate to steep	449935
2	Ballure Glen and Reservoir	Easy	457935
3	Ballaglass Glen	Easy	467897
4	Dhoon Glen	Steep in places	455864
5	Tholt e Will Glen	Easy to moderate	386881
6	Laxey Glen (and Glen Roy)	Easy (to moderate)	432843
7	Bishopscourt Glen	Easy	328925
8	Glen Wyllin and Cooildary	Easy	315903
9	Glen Mooar (by Kirk Michael)	Easy to moderate	305894
10	Glen Helen	Easy	295843
11	Bibaloe Walk and Mollie Quirk's Glen	Easy	405786
12	Groudle Glen	Easy	420784
13	Port Soderick Glen	Easy	346727
14	Silverdale Glen	Easy	275710
15	Glen Maye	Easy to moderate	236798
16	Colby Glen	Easy	231710
17	Bradda Glen	Easy	195697
	OTHER GLEN WALKS – COUNTRYSIDE		
A	Glen Shoggle	Easy to moderate	352919
B	Glen Dhoo	Easy	352919
C	Cornaa Glen	Easy	467897
D	Glen Mooar (by Glen Maye)	Easy	235798
	OTHER GLEN WALKS – TOWN		
E	Port Jack Glen	Easy	399773
F	Summerhill Glen (floodlit at night)	Easy	389778
G	Glen Falcon	Easy	380766
H	Athol Park Glen	Easy	195689

Contents

Map of Location of Glen Walks 2

Index of Glen Walks 3

Introduction 4

Walk Descriptions – Manx National Glens

Walk 1: Elfin Glen / Lhergy Frissel 9

Walk 2: Ballure Glen and Reservoir 11

Walk 3: Ballaglas Glen 13

Walk 4: Dhoon Glen 14

Walk 5: Tholt e Will Glen 16

Walk 6: Laxey Glen (and Glen Roy) 17

Walk 7: Bishopscourt Glen 20

Walk 8: Glen Wyllin (and Cooildary) 21

Walk 9: Glen Moaar (by Kirk Michael) 23

Walk 10: Glen Helen 25

Walk 11: Bibaloe Walk and Mollie Quirk's Glen 28

Walk 12: Groudle Glen 29

Walk 13: Port Soderick Glen 31

Walk 14: Silverdale Glen 32

Walk 15: Glen Maye 35

Walk 16: Colby Glen 36

Walk 17: Bradda Glen 37

Walk Descriptions – Other Glen Walks

Walk A: Glen Shoggle 40

Walk B: Glen Dhoo 41

Walk C: Cornaa Glen 42

Walk D: Glen Mooar (by Glen Maye) 44

Walk E: Port Jack Glen 45

Walk F: Summerhill Glen (floodlit at night) 46

Walk G: Glen Falcon 47

Walk H: Athol Park Glen 48

Introduction

Splendour of the Manx glens

For such a small place, the Isle of Man has a great number of scenic and exciting glens to explore, each with its own uniqueness. From the bluebell-rich Ballaglass Glen in the north, the deeply cavernous fern-covered Glen Maye in the west, the wonderful sea cliff panoramas of Bradda Glen in the south to the towering waterfall of Dhoon Glen in the east. Some glens are extensive areas in the heart of the countryside and can take a few hours to explore completely; others are small, quiet oases of tranquillity in the centre of towns. Many contain unusual buildings and features which date back to their Victorian origins or earlier, others have modern carved trees which tell stories of wizards and fairies. And one, Summerhill Glen, comes to life after darkness falls.

This book of 25 walks includes all 18 Manx National Glens which are maintained in their original semi-natural state by the Government. Many of these were enhanced with extensive tree and flowering bush plantings in the late Victorian era to attract the growing number of people who visited Isle of Man on holiday. Additional walks are included along entirely natural glen-valleys in the countryside often passing through remote areas. A small number of public glens in towns that have been specifically designed and landscaped as places of peace and interest to enjoy are also described in this book.

The walks are generally short (about 4 miles is the longest complete walk) with easy-to-follow and well-kept footpaths. Most are across easy terrain perhaps with an occasional moderate climb or flight of steps. A couple have some steep sections (indicated in Index of Glen Walks). All are easily accessed by car and the majority can be reached by public transport.

Glens are open throughout the year (free of charge). Spring and summer are good seasons for walking as the trees and other plants will be at their best. Autumn has the highlight of the myriad of different colours of the leaves, and winter snow and frost can transform the landscape. Certain sections of paths are quite close to the river level and so can become muddy after periods of heavy rain.

Using this book

This guide describes a total of 25 walks. 17 are Manx National Glens – there are 18 of these, however Elfin Glen and Lhergy Frissel are combined in one walk. Four are in open countryside following a river along a wooded valley or forest. A further four walks are in public glens, maintained by the town in which they are located: these are generally smaller and ornamental rather than having the more natural appearance of the National Glens. The Index of Glen Walks summarises the terrain of each walk, with the OS map grid reference of the glen entrance.

All glens have easy to follow paths which are generally well maintained. The main section comprises detailed descriptions of how to follow a suggested walk in each glen, where to look out for turnings and pointing out interesting views and old buildings. The walk descriptions start and finish at the same place and are designed to take you round the full extent of each glen. However, many glens have a network of paths which can be used to explore the area in your own way. The descriptions note if a certain section is prone to being particularly wet or muddy, so you can 'reserve' them for dry weather or wear the appropriate gear.

Groudle Glen

Route descriptions have brief sections that describe the history of, or interesting stories about, the area or features or monuments that are passed on the walk. There is information on reaching the start of the walk by car or using public transport (if appropriate).

Practical information before you set off

As many glens have fast-flowing rivers running through them, paths can occasionally be damaged by flooding and landslips following heavy rains, or fallen tress after strong winds. This may necessitate some of the paths being closed temporarily (although this can leave other paths perfectly useable). Department of Environment Food and Agriculture (Forestry Division) are responsible for path maintenance in Manx National Glens – telephone 01624 695701.

For many glens it is not necessary to have a map to follows the paths: however, for some which cover larger areas it can be helpful. But it is always useful to have a map to find the start point of the walk and to have an appreciation of the surrounding countryside and coast.

I find the OS Landranger Map Sheet 95 (scale 1:50,000 or 1.25 inches to one mile) is the most practical for travelling to the glen and does provide some direction information for navigating the larger glens. If you have a current version of OS Landranger Sheet 95 you can download a digital version of the map onto your smartphone or tablet. I recommend this as in my experience it also shows where one is with relative accuracy.

The more detailed Isle of Man Survey Outdoor Leisure Map (scale 1:25,000 or 2.5 inches to one mile) generally has better coverage of the paths themselves, although it is occasionally possible that it is out of date.

Public transport

If you are using public transport, consulting the latest bus timetable will be important in planning how to reach the start of a day's walk and how to return at the end. Bus routes and times are available at www.bus.im or on 01624 662525 or a printed timetable is available from the Visitor Centre in the Sea Terminal (Douglas) or other visitor attractions.

In addition many walks can be accessed by heritage railway services that were established in the Victorian era to cater for the booming summer holiday visitor trade. The Manx Electric Railway (MER) runs from Douglas northwards along the east coast passing through Laxey and terminates in Ramsey. The Steam Railway runs from Douglas southwards passing through Castletown and ending at Port Erin. They run seasonally (spring and summer) – routes and times are available at the abovementioned places.

Contactless payment is taken on all services, as well as cash. 'Go cards' are available which allow unlimited use of bus and train services for set number of days at discounted rates. In each section of this book bus information is summarised, but not in any detail as routes and schedules do change.

Weather

Checking the weather in advance is advised for any walk. There can be few people who enjoy walking in the rain if it can be avoided – although the tree canopies of many glens can provide some protection from the elements. All the Island radio stations and news websites carry weather forecasts for one to two days ahead. I find the most detailed is on http://www.bbc.co.uk/weather/3042237 which gives hour-by-hour forecasts for the next day.

What to wear?

Ordinary flat-soled shoes or trainers are suitable for most walks indicated as 'easy'. For those described as 'moderate' or 'steep' outdoor walking trainers with good grip on the sole are fine.

Happy glen walking.

8

Dhoon Glen

1. Elfin Glen and Lhergy Frissel

OS Map ref. start: 449935
Terrain: Moderate with several relatively steep sections
Access: On the Mountain Road (A18) just to the south of Ramsey there is parking on the outside of the Hairpin. From Bus / Manx Electric Railway stations in Ramsey walk up May Hill to the Hairpin.

A woodland walk in Elfin Glen between two famous locations on TT course, return is a walk through Lhergy Frissel to Albert Tower, panoramic views of Ramsey and the north.

Originally called Ballacowle Glen, it was given the English name Elfin Glen in mid-19th century to attract holidaymakers. Proceed up the wooden steps, turn right along a rough path uphill. Cross a small bridge with river on the left, the path continues upwards and bends left. At a junction with another path detour right to a wooden viewing platform overlooking Ramsey and the coastline stretching northwards. Return back to the junction and continue forwards, the path climbs and now the stream is a considerable distance below on the left.

The path slopes down to a small bridge, then up the steps with the gorge on the left as one heads down river. Pass through a gap in the wall. Turn right to head uphill. The path leaves the cover of woodland and becomes more grassed over, the slopes of North Barrule appear in front. Cross a short wooden walkway, then up a few stone steps to reach the Mountain Road. The famous Gooseneck bend is a few hundred yards down the road on the left – but as this can be a busy and fast road it is advised to take great care if walking to this TT Course landmark. Retrace one's steps

View north from Albert Tower

descending past the gap in the wall, this section has many loose stones and exposed tree roots so proceed with caution.

At the meeting of paths bear right to follow the route signed the Albert Tower. Pass through a derelict kissing-gate and follow the track on the right climbing steeply uphill through the trees. As one leaves the cover of the trees the path levels off and one can see a communication mast which is attempting to hide its true identity with artificial vegetation. The path continues level and straight as Albert Tower comes into view.

The Albert Tower. This was built to commemorate the visit of Prince Albert in 1847. He climbed to the top of the hill lead by the town's barber, who was pressed into action as a guide at short notice (the Royal party's arrival was totally unexpected), and was followed by a crowd of curious locals From the summit, which was thereafter named Albert Mount, he viewed the town of Ramsey and the northern plain. The tower is 45 feet high and made from slate and granite but, unfortunately, it is not usually open. The now fading plaque reads 'Erected on the spot where HRH Prince Albert stood to view Ramsey and its neighbourhood during the visit of Her Most Gracious Majesty, Queen Victoria to Ramsey Bay on XXth September MDCCCLVII'.

Dramatic views open up of Ramsey Bay, the sandy beach stretching northwards for miles and the northern plain with the villages of Jurby, Andreas and Bride. The path continues with views on the right of North Barrule and the ribbon-like Mountain Road. On the far side there are views east to Maughold Head and, on a clear day, over to the Lakeland Fells.

Return to the Hairpin by retracing one's steps to the junction of paths where one bears right to follow the path downhill and take the steps to the car parking area.

Claughbane Woods. The adjacent Claughbane is predominantly coniferous woodland and has been worked as a commercial plantation for many years. The woods to the east are managed purely for recreation and scenic value. A slate quarry used to exist on the site and it is this slate that was used in building the Albert Tower.

Albert Tower

2. Ballure Glen and Reservoir

OS Map ref. start: 457935
Terrain: Easy
Access: There is on-street parking along side roads to the south of Ramsey off the coast road (A2). Ramsey Manx Electric railway (MER) and bus stations are about ½ mile from the start of the walk.

A walk up to and round a picturesque little reservoir, then down through the glen through a hidden gem by the beach.

Walk away from the town along the right hand pavement of the coast road and cross the MER tracks. Immediately bear right up a tarmac road, signed as a public footpath to the Gooseneck, which leads up to the reservoir. The road crosses a bridge with the stream now on the right. On the left is a small former reservoir which was found to be inadequate to supply the fast-growing Ramsey during the tourism boom of late 19th century. Take the track that ascends steeply on the right to the reservoir dam wall.

There is an information board about the locality which shows various walking routes. A recommended walk is to proceed anti-clockwise on the reservoir perimeter path which is through the gate to the immediate right of the information board. There is a well-made gravel path with occasional steps to take one over the streams that flow into the reservoir. A significant flight of steps take you up into the woodland with great views down to the water. The path levels off then drops down a few steps and turns left through a gate to return to the reservoir dam wall.

Now follow the footpath sign and take a track through a gate that leads up to the woods. Pass by a small path on the left. Just before the blue gate there are some steps and a path on the left which leads up to a picnic area and, eventually, the TT Course (retrace one's steps to continue the glen walk). Proceed through the gate, continuing straight down along the path.

Ballure Reservoir

The glen was created by the Ramsey Water Company after their waterworks was opened in 1885. It was privately owned for several decades until it was sold to the Forestry Board in 1959. The path slopes gently downhill through the trees, where the path levels there are delightful glades to the left. The path is lined with wild garlic in the spring: this plant has contributed to the town's name, as the Manx for Ramsey is *Rhumsaa* which translates as 'wild garlic river'.

After the path hairpins right it emerges on to the Ramsey road by the MER track: immediately cross the road and take a narrow path on the right where there is a gap in the wall. Follow this path, there are short flights of concrete steps, to reach the river. The slightly uneven track follows the river which soon goes through a charming archway and reaches the sea. Turn left along the beach and in a couple of hundred yards there are concrete steps leading up to a track past the gates of a house. Take the path on the left to emerge on to the main road, turn right to head towards Ramsey.

Ballure Walk

3. Ballaglass Glen

OS Map ref. start: 467897
Terrain: Easy
Access: A few miles south of Ramsey on the coast road (A2) turn left onto A15 at the Hibernian, after a mile take the first right which leads across Manx Electric Railway (MER) tracks to a car park on the right by the glen entrance. There are MER stops at Cornaa (for main entrance) and Ballaglass Glen (upper glen entrance).

An idyllic glen walk following the spectacular Cornaa river, numerous waterfalls and trails for children to follow. (Cornaa Glen is a convenient walk while one is here).

Ballaglass Glen. The glen was acquired by the Forestry Board in 1952 from its previous owner The Manx Electric Railway Company who had been developing it to encourage visits by MER passengers. The name Ballaglass translates as *'Farm of the stream'*. The Great Mona Mining Company, which extracted lead, zinc and copper, operated here in the 1850's and 1860's.

There is an information board at the entrance which shows several paths, this route is one of the longer ones taking in many of the glen's features. Cross the wide footbridge and proceed through the gate on the left and along a broad path sloping uphill with the perimeter of the glen nearby on the right. This is the 'Wizzard of Mann' trail. Bear right keeping close to the glen perimeter. When the path forks bear left (right hand fork takes one away from the glen towards Ballaglass Glen MER station). Proceed forwards ignoring the stepped path on the left, passing a derelict white building: this is a corn mill last used in 1951.

Continue on towards the sound of rushing water, the path takes one close to the river. At the time of writing the path across on the other side of the river was closed for repair, but is recommended to explore the glen further. (After returning) retrace one's steps to the derelict building to follow a route by the river. The route descends using a handrail in places, trees occasionally squeeze the path to be extremely narrow. There are steps and a handrail to take one closer to the river by a waterfall. Keep to the lower level path, pass a bench by a series of water cascades. At another bridge keep to this side of the river (the path across the bridge leads up away from the river).

At a fork take the path to the right to continue the route close to the river. Immediately past a bench take a flight of steps on the left indicated by the Wizzard sign which leads up to a little cottage with a carving of our wizard from a tree trunk (note that he is a 'living' entity as there are fungi growing on him!). Continue straight on past the cottage, the path winds through the trees and eventually leads towards the entrance gate and the car park.

The Cornaa Glen walk is accessed from this car park.

Ballaglass Glen

4. Dhoon Glen

OS Map ref. start: 455864
Terrain: Steep in several places
Access: Take the coast road (A2) northwards from Laxey until you reach Dhoon Glen Halt (Manx Electric Railway). There is ample parking in the lay-by. There are bus and MER stops.

An impressive glen following a stream down to Dhoon Bay, there is a spectacular waterfall and interesting public art on the beach. It is a steep walk with a descent of 560 feet and over 190 steps on the return.

Dhoon Glen. Named Glion y Dowin in Manx, it is the steepest Manx glen but it amply rewards one's effort. Jenkinson wrote in his tour guide in 1874 *"They are undoubtedly the largest and most beautiful cascades on the island, but hitherto they have been very little known. They are deeply recessed in a romantic and well-wooded glen"*. There are the remains of a lead mine from mid-19th century: it was never profitable so the owner sold and leased land to James Quilleash who began to develop the glen for visitors. By early 1880s the glen had refreshment rooms, stabling, a hotel and an inn. The Manx Fairy, a small passenger ship, used to run daily between Douglas and Ramsey calling at Dhoon Bay to unload passengers, who spent the day on the beach or in the glen, before being picked up for the return journey. With the arrival of the MER in 1897 the glen was taken over by the company who charged 4d admission of which the owners received 1 3/4d. Its popularity waned after WWII and

the Forestry Board purchased the glen in 1955.

Cross the MER line to the hut and immediately to its right there are concrete steps leading down past public conveniences to join a path that goes by the side of the stream. There is a flight of steps down, then a wooden walkway and another short flight of steps. The path passes under a bridge and reaches a section with a wooden handrail
(Alternatively one can take the minor road a few hundred yards and just beyond the Raad ny Foillan way-marker there is a gate and footpath sign for Dhoon Beach. The path heads left downhill through trees to reach a wooden fence/hand rail).
Turn right downhill following the handrail for the

Public art on Dhoon Beach

best views of the valley and stream below. As this comes to an end proceed down the path that is slightly away from the edge. Pick your way carefully as the surface is uneven and can be muddy in places due to rainwater run-off. The path heads uphill briefly towards the remains of a chimney and a building which housed a large wheel that pumped water out of the mine.

Proceed along the path and at a bench it forks, take the left branch where there are steps down for close-up views of the waterfalls. The first part is the smaller section where water tumbles over the rocks with views upstream of trees that have fallen over and now span the channel. The path hugs the side of the stream and through gaps in the trees you begin to notice the Irish Sea in the distance. Ferns and mosses cover the cliffs on the right giving it a carpet-like feel to the touch.

As the sound of the rushing water grows one comes to a T-junction – take the left path and zig-zagging down a second, taller section of the waterfall comes into view. (The right path is an old pack horse track - a higher level route which by-passes the second part of the waterfall and joins the main trail lower down the valley). The waterfall is known as the *Inneen Vooar* or 'Big Girl' and is one of the highest on the Island falling over 130 feet (40 metres) in the two drops. In Manx folklore there is a story of a young girl who had been drowned in the pool below the waterfall, and it is said that her ghost haunts the glen.

Cross an old stone bridge so the stream is now on the right. There are a succession of modern bridges which snakes the path from one side of the river to the other and back. The path spills out onto Dhoon Beach and in the distance, on a clear day, you can make out the Lakeland Fells. At the time of writing, flat stones and pebbles had been balanced on top of each other on the beach to create mini towers some as tall as three feet. The overall effect is a wonderful display of spontaneous popular art.

Return by the same route.

Dhoon Glen

5. Tholt e Will Glen

OS Map ref. start: 386881
Terrain: Easy with some moderately steep sections
Access: Take the A14 from the Mountain Road
(A18) at the Bungalow to the bottom of Sulby Valley.
There is a car park near the glen entrance. There is
no convenient public transport.

*A woodland walk with steepling views down Sulby
valley and delightful waterfalls.*

Tholt e Will Glen. The name is derived from
Tolta-yn-wooliae which is Celtic for 'hill of the
cattlefold'. This became the first National Glen
when it was purchased from the Manx
Electric Railway Company by the Forestry
Board in 1952. The MER had acquired the
land earlier as an attraction to encourage
visitors to use the Snaefell Mountain Railway,
which was one of the principal ways of
reaching it. At the height of the tourism boom
in the 1890s there was a hotel, tearooms and a
'museum of Manx curiosities' in the glen.

Walk to the wooden gate and bridge across the
river to enter the glen. The Sulby River is the longest
river on the Island at just over 11 miles. It rises at
the top of the valley between Snaefell and Beinn-y-
Phott and flows into Sulby Reservoir and then heads
to Ramsey. The river's flow is regulated by the
reservoir so, unless it is full and there is an
overflow, the river is not always as awesome a sight
as it might be.

Follow the path to the right passing a house and
garden on the right, continue along the main track
ignoring a steep path on the left. Cross over the
bridge, the path ascends with the stream on the
left. The path becomes steeper and hairpins left and
right. Reach a left turn – carrying on uphill leads to
the upper exit of the glen – which one takes using
steps down to continue the circuit. Cross over the
stream by the bridge, pausing to take in the steep
ribbon waterfall on the right as it plunges into a
crystal clear plunge pool. Take the steps to go up
into the trees, soon the path levels off as one walks
across a carpet of pine needles – these trees were
mainly planted in mid-20th century. Just in front of
a small red and white marker post bear left
downhill, after a flight of steps the path levels off.

When one reaches a wider path bear left
downhill with a wall on the right. Turn right when it
exits out onto the path which was used on the
outward section and return to the car park.

Sulby River

6. Laxey Glen (leading to Glen Roy)

OS Map ref. start: 432843
Terrain: Easy, occasionally moderately steep
Access: The glen is located in Laxey on the main coast road (A2): heading north, immediately after the bridge by the Laxey Flour Mill there is a turning on the left, signed Laxey Glen, which leads up to a car park. Laxey has bus and Manx Electric Railway stops.

This is a picturesque walk beside the Laxey River in a former pleasure garden. For the more adventurous the path continues into Glen Roy (and Axnfell Plantation). The paths can be muddy following wet weather. Easy walking, occasionally moderately steep in Glen Roy.

Laxey Glen Gardens. This area was actively managed from 1800s when the Reverend William Fitzsimmons began a planting programme: a few of the larger trees date from this period. To capitalise on the boom in tourism the Glen Gardens were opened as a public leisure area known as Victoria Park in the 1860s – it accommodated a host of attractions and a pavilion. The Gardens were an extensive visitor attraction judging by this description in 1881 *'containing, among other attractions and amusements, pleasant and secluded walks, bowers, and rustic seats, swings, quoits, and hobby horses, croquet, lawn tennis, bowling green, American bowling saloon, and everything needful to enable visitors to spend a most enjoyable day'.* The decline in tourism resulted in the glen being sold to the Forestry Board in 1956.

Follow the road past the Pavilion which houses a café, bistro and bar. Take the path into the glen itself: on the left is a flat lawn that was originally used for croquet or bowls. Continue on the right path, it hairpins down flights of steps to, and crosses, the river which is now on one's right. There are public toilets: on the left is Laxey Flour Mill. The right hand path follows the Laxey River through the trees: notice a log on the left carved in the shape of a crocodile. In the river bed there are debris catchers which aim to prevent tree branches and rocks from being pushed down the river during storms and floods. In the past such debris has contributed to Lower Laxey being flooded and a bridge being damaged.

Proceed over a low stile in a gap in the wall: this probably marked the end of Laxey Glen, so one is now in Glen Roy. The path climbs a little above the river but soon descends. Exposed river banks on the far side are evidence of erosion during recent storms. The river level path stops so take the route uphill. After a while the path becomes concreted with a low wall on either side. The path now becomes a little more challenging to walk. At the time of writing, just after the bridge a section of the riverside path has slipped away stopping further progress up Glen Roy. The only path is up through Axnfell Plantation.

Return by the same route. When reaching the crocodile carving one can cross the river and head across to a flight of stone steps and follow the path back to the café.

Laxey River

Bishopscourt Glen

7. Bishopscourt Glen

OS Map ref. start: 328925
Terrain: Easy
Access: Follow the A3 (TT Course) north from Kirk Michael. After about 1½ miles Bishops Court (the Bishop's former residence) is on the left, opposite this is a small lay-by close to the glen entrance. It is on a regular bus route.

A woodland walk with luxuriant vegetation and several places of interest including a cave, two ponds and a model of Tynwald Hill.

Bishopscourt Glen. It is situated across the road from the former residence of the Bishop of Sodor and Man. In the late 17th and early 18th centuries Bishop Wilson arranged the planting of several thousand trees to form the glen as his private garden. It was owned privately until it was bought by the Forestry Board in 1963.

The entrance is a black wooden gate between two white gateposts bearing the Bishop's coat-of-arms: there is an information board. The route which circles the glen clockwise begins with the path on the left. This section of the walk has a profusion of spring bulbs and flowering wild garlic. Keep the river on the right, ignoring the small footbridge, as the path climbs gradually. There is a pond on the right usually with a large flock of ducks. Keep on the low level path, not taking the sloping walkway on the left.

The next section has a profusion of rhododendrons which flower in the summer. Cross over the river at two places (stone slabs) still taking the lower level path that follows closer to the river. Cross a wooden bridge, pass another bridge on the right – a notched seat has been carved from the branch of a tree that has fallen over. The path steepens slightly. By a wooden retaining wall to the

right is a small path up to a cave. Known as the 'Cave of the Winds', it is where Bishop Murray allegedly took refuge from angry locals at the time of the Potato Tithe Riots in 1825.

Return to the path climbing uphill, and cross a stone bridge so that the river on is on the left. After a short flight of steps the path now bends back on the return loop. Cross the wooden bridge with the path bearing right, walk through a delightful archway made by a curved tree trunk. Path descends to cross the river and take a flight of steps and over a bridge. Turn left briefly onto the path used in the outward part of the route. At the next stone bridge, bear left following a cinder track. Pass a small pond on the right and the larger pond from the outward journey.

The path forks left down a couple of steps to a wooden bridge, follow the path on the right to reach Mount Aeolus. This was built as a replica of Tynwald Hill in St Johns, where an open air parliament is held on Tynwald Day (early July). The mound was built to commemorate the victory of an English fleet against the French off the coast of the Island in 1760. *'The Aeolus'* was the name of the Royal Navy ship which lead the attack.

Return to the gate to leave the glen.

8. Glen Wyllin and Cooildarry

OS Map ref. start: 315903
Terrain: Easy
Access: Glen Whyllin is located just south of Kirk Michael on the Peel coast road (A4). There is parking in the campsite. There is a bus stop in Kirk Michael.

Glen Whyllin is a wooded area leading down to the coast (campsite has public access). Across the road Cooildarry is a nature reserve with a variety of trees and shrubs set in the valley of a stream.

Glen Wyllin. Glen Wyllin translates into English as 'Glen of the mill'. It was opened to the public as the Glen Wyllin Pleasure Grounds in 1890. The glen was a thriving attraction for several decades offering a range of amusements for a three pence charge for adults. From 1907 it was run by the Kinvig family who were staunch Methodists so it was closed on Sundays. Visitors could hire bathing costumes, hats and towels and the use of a bathing hut. Amusements consisted of croquet, putting, bowls, tennis, children's swings, a boating lake and a hobbyhorse roundabout. It was acquired by the Isle of Man Railway Company in 1935 (there used to be a station in Kirk Michael) and continued as a successful tourist attraction until 1950s. It fell into disrepair and was acquired by the Forestry Board in 1978.

Walk down through the campsite to the coast. This part of the coast is subject to erosion as the cliffs are simply glacial deposit sand. In 1991/92 large blocks of granite were placed along the bottom of the cliffs to stop erosion. However, it seems to have simply transferred the problem along the coast.

Return inland and by the old railway bridge support tower, follow the wooden rail on the right towards the woodland and, at the end, turn left to take a path that runs along the edge of the trees.

Keep to the low level path, climb a flight of steps and cross the road carefully. Just to the right of the road sign is a Manx Wildlife Trust footpath which could be muddy in places if it has been raining recently (alternatively there is a wider track which leads in the same direction).

The path passes behind cottages and skirts woodland whose floor is carpeted with bluebell, primrose, wood anemone and wild garlic in the spring. There is an abundance of rhododendron that flowers later in the year. There is a small footbridge as the path crosses a wider track: pause at the information board before you enter the nature reserve.

Cooildarry Nature Reserve. The reserve is managed by the Manx Wildlife Trust: the name is derived from the Manx Gaelic darragh (oak tree) and cooil (nook). Much of the woodland was planted in the Victorian era – as were many other Manx glens. The tree species are varied with elm, ash, alder, sycamore and beech being dominant. There are also exotic species such as rhododendron and cherry laurel. Mosses and ferns all grow in profusion in the moist shady conditions. In springtime the ground is carpeted with primrose, wood anemone, wood sorrel, lesser celandine and bluebell.

The path proceeds downhill through trees, continue past the footbridge up and down flights of steps and over wooden walking boards. It reaches the top of a cliff with the river about 30 feet below. Continue to a bridge, turn left (at time of writing the right hand path is cordoned off after a few hundred yards). Cross another bridge and on the left is the cliff that the path had reached previously. At a fork head right uphill passing a waterfall on the right through the trees. In the grass on the right is a stone tablet marking the site of a Fuller's Earth works, the remains of the works are obscured by trees on the other side of the path. Fuller's Earth is a calcium-based clay that is fine, off-white and highly absorbent. It was extracted from the glacial deposits in this area and used as an important ingredient in absorbing and removing oil from sheep's wool. It is also used as an inert substance in artillery shells.

The path climbs away from the river and finishes by a gate which leads on to the main road. Retrace one's steps, cross over the bridge and turn right to return on the path that was used initially and return to the entrance. From here either take the wider track on the right or the narrower path on the left. Turn right along the road to return to Kirk Michael for the bus stop or straight across for the campsite.

This walk can be combined with the nearby Glen Mooar walk by following the Raad ny Foillan left along the beach: this walk connects the lower end of Glen Whyllin with Glen Mooar.

Glen Wyllin looking towards Slieau Freoaghane

Glen Wyllin

9. Glen Mooar (by Kirk Michael)

OS Map ref. start: 305894
Terrain: Easy, moderately steep in a few places
Access: The glen can be accessed on the Peel-Kirk Michael coast road (A4) about one mile south of Kirk Michael. There is a car park down the narrow road on the right (cross over the ford). It is on a bus route.

A woodland walk following an upper level path (lower level closed at time of writing) with remains of an ancient keeill and an impressive waterfall. Glen Mooar also extends down to the sea.

Start by following the route west from the main road / car park to the beach. This follows a narrow road with a footbridge across a stream, it passes the car park (toilet available) before leading out to the beach. Return along this route, cross the road and proceed through the gate by the Raad ny Foillan way-marker to enter Glen Mooar.

At the time of writing the lower levels of the glen cannot be accessed but the higher level route is open. Continue past the towers that used to carry the Steam Railway linking St John's, Kirk Michael and Ramsey. The two pillars are 70ft high and were built in 1878, they used to support a railway bridge over the glen. Carry straight on past the blue way-marker which points right. The path winds uphill through the woodland. Keep on the main path as it turns left and descends by a bench. On the left are the remains of St Patrick's Chapel (*Cabbal Pherick*) in a clearing.

Cabbal Pherick (St Patrick's Chapel). All that remains of this 8th–10th century chapel is the low rectangular wall, surrounded by the remains of an outer wall which probably would have encompassed a burial area. The altar would have been at the east end of the chapel facing the Holy Land. Itinerant priests would have visited the site and people from nearby settlements would gather for a service that would have been held from the doorway at the western end. The chapel is named after the Irish Saint who, legend has it, was the first to preach the Christian word on the Isle of Man. It is probably significant that the chapel was located close to a waterfall as this may have held special significance to those living in the area.

In a couple of hundred yards proceed through a gap in a grassed wall on the left, there is a flight of steps leading down to the river and waterfall named Spooyt Vane (Manx Gaelic for white spout). This is one of the highest and most photographed waterfalls on the Island. Return up the steps and retrace one's steps back to the glen entrance.

This walk can be combined with the nearby Glen Wyllin & Cooildary walk by following the Raad ny Foillan right along the beach which connects the lower end of Glen Mooar with Glen Whyllin.

Spooyt Vane

10. Glen Helen

OS Map ref. start: 295843
Terrain: Easy
Access: On the A3 to Kirk Michael, the large Glen Helen car park is on the right about 2½ miles from Ballacraine crossroads. There is no bus service.

A walk through varied and scenic woodland by a river running through a deep gorge with an attractive waterfall. There is a restaurant / café by the entrance and public toilets.

Glen Helen. One of the best known of the Island's glens, Glen Helen was created in the 1860s by a consortium of Manx businessmen who laid its paths, carried out extensive planting of trees and ornamental shrubs and constructed river bridges. It was opened to the public in 1867 for a small charge (originally four pence). It was initially known as *Glen* Rhenass, the name of the river flowing through it, but was re-named after a lady in the life of the then owner John Marsden. It was subsequently taken over by the Government in 1958. There is a variety of impressive trees including sequoia, thuja, spruces, Douglas fir, oak, sycamore and beech which give a beautiful variegated appearance.

There is an information board by the entrance – unfortunately at the time of writing there is no complete return path along the south side. Behind the café there is a small camp site with wooden cabins. Proceed along the tarmac road past the old Swiss House restaurant and toilets, nearby is a restored fountain which is nearly 150 years old. In 1933 the famous lady flyer Amy Johnson visited the glen and to mark the occasion she planted a Douglas fir, which is adjacent to the fountain.

The main path keeps the river on the right – one can cross over by bridge but certain stretches of the path on this side were closed at the time of writing. Following storms a few trees have fallen over and some lie across the river. The path is wide and is well-maintained: gradually it takes one higher away from the river providing wonderful views.

There is a bridge and viewing platform over the river by the Rhenass Waterfall. After stopping to admire the spectacle continue along a narrow path up a flight of steps. Just beyond the handrail take the stepped path on the left and proceed towards the wooden railings. You are now directly above the main waterfall which can be heard but not seen. Walk round a little further to see a torrent of water rushing on its way between the rocks. Return back to the narrow path and continue up the glen. On the right a path leads downwards nearer the river, in time there is a small wooden bridge which crosses the river and leads on to a path with the river now on the right.

Follow this path down the valley until a wooden bridge which crosses back to the viewing platform (the path that continues with the river on one's right was closed at the time of writing). Return along the original path until near the end of the glen, take the bridge over the river – immediately in front there looks to be a grand throne made from rocks. Turn right and the path leads to a children's playground and a final bridge to return to the car park.

Victorian Fountain

Glen Helen

11. Bibaloe Walk and Mollie Quirk's Glen

OS Map ref. start: 405786
Terrain: Easy, occasionally moderately steep
Access: Take the main road (A2) north from Onchan, after a dip in the road there is a lay-by on the left for parking. Onchan is served by buses from Douglas.

The entrances to both Bibaloe Walk and Molly Quirk's Glen are at the lay-by. Bibaloe is pleasant short walk in woods by a stream. Mollie Quirk's is much larger glen with many routes either lower along the heavily wooded Groudle River or higher up a little above the trees.

The entrance gate to Bibaloe is the higher one on the right. The path proceeds gradually uphill through the trees with the stream on the left. It ends at the gate leading on to the main road just before

Mollie Quirk's Glen

the turning for Ballakilmartin. Retrace one's steps to the lower entrance.

Take the middle gate to enter Molly Quirk's Glen by a footbridge across the stream (the route will return via the lower gate).

Molly Quirk's Glen. The glen is named after Molly Quirk who was known to have considerable wealth and who was robbed and murdered in the glen. There have reputedly been sightings of her ghost wandering in the glen. The Forestry Department purchased the glen in 1955 for £100 (worth just over £2,500 in today's money). It was bought from the trustees of Stephen and Margaret Quirk – unsure if the lady was the same person referred to in the legend!

After a few yards bear right uphill past a bench and soon one is above the treeline with views across the rooftops of Onchan and out across Douglas Bay. When the edge of the field is reached the path descends, take the stepped path of to the left (the forward path soon becomes overgrown and difficult to walk). In a few hundred yards at a junction of paths turn right heading to a bridge across the river. Climb a few steps to follow a path with the river on the left – one can now turn right to follow the path to the top end of the glen. A right turn takes one further up, with the river below now, until a main road is reached by a bridge.

Retrace one's steps and continue on the path passing the bridge. The path generally descends but there are occasional steps upward. Cross over a concrete water channel and carry on forwards, by a cut-down tree trunk take the path left to cross the river. Bear right and up the steps to return to the lay-by by the lower entrance.

Mollie Quirk's Glen does continue into Groudle Glen thanks to the underpass beneath the main road. To access this, instead of crossing the river on the bridge continue forwards.

12. Groudle Glen

OS Map ref. start: 420784
Terrain: Easy
Access: From the northern end of Douglas Promenade take A11 following the Manx Electric Railway (MER). Turn right down Groudle Old Road, also signed Groudle Beach, and park in the car park at the foot of the hill. There are bus and MER stops nearby.

There are three different and interesting experiences to be had here – Port Groudle, the miniature steam railway and the glen walk itself.

Groudle Glen. In 1890 an entrepreneur, Richard Maltby Broadbent, purchased the lease to the whole area here. At that time the glen was in its natural state with grass, ferns and very few trees, indeed when the glen first opened to the public it was known as 'The Fern Glen of the Isle of Man'. He landscaped it, built a hotel, café and other facilities to transform it into a major tourist attraction. He persuaded the company responsible for the electric railway to build the track near the glen with a station opposite the hotel – in exchange for a percentage of the glen's admission charge.

From the car park take the path towards to the beach known as Port Groudle. The beach has been formed by the continuous action of storm tides that bring up pebbles and rocks from the sea bed and hurl them up to form the bank. The shape of the beach is changing constantly in response to the power of the sea. During periods of high tide one can see waves heading upstream, seemingly against the flow of the river, up to and beyond the bridge.

Retrace one's steps, cross the river on the wooden bridge and follow the steps up the slope to approach the railway track and a stop named North Pole Halt. When not in use one can walk alongside

the track beyond the Halt along the cliff top towards the Sea Lion Rocks Terminus. Beyond this one can see the remains of open air pools.

Groudle Glen Railway. It is a 2 foot gauge railway which was built in 1896 to attract visitors to the glen and transport them to man-made pools which housed sea lions and bears until early in the 20th century. The sea lions were looked after until the outbreak of World War II when they were let into the sea. The railway fell into disrepair in the 1960s. In 1982 volunteers started work on the railway and it was re-opened to the public in 1986. It usually operates on Sundays from April to October with occasional evening services in the summer.

On the left of the halt by the blue footpath sign there is a flight of steps down to a path that skirts the woods and leads you into the glen itself. On the

Gandalf

right is a huge tank which has been creatively painted. By side of the path a tree trunk has been carved to represent Gandalf from Lord of the Rings.

After a few minutes there is a path on the right leading up to the Lhen Coan Station. The station is attractively designed and has advertising signs from a bygone era. Beyond the end of the tracks there is a path going up to the top of the glen and eventually leading on to the main road. This gives some wonderful views down to the stream and the occasional waterfall.

For the main glen walk return down the steps to the river and cross the bridge. This path passes a bandstand which has been rebuilt on the site of the original one, only much smaller. A little further on there is a water-wheel known as the 'Little Isabella' (a reference to the Laxey Wheel named 'Lady Isabella'). It was built in 1894 with the original purpose of powering the fairy lights and pumping water up to the Groudle Hotel on the main road. It was restored in 2020.

Immediately beyond this there is a narrow and deep gorge. As the path widens an impressive viaduct towers over the glen: this was built so that the MER could extend beyond Groudle to Laxey. The path that hairpins left leads to the top entrance of the glen where the hotel was originally situated, and Groudle Station where MER trains still stop. From here one can either follow the main road left back down to the turning for Groudle Beach. Or return

down to the glen to continue to follow the path by the river.

Further along the main glen path there is evidence of storm damage with felled trees lying across the river. The path continues using a series of raised wooden walkways and crosses over a couple of bridges. The main road is soon reached where Groudle Glen formally ends. However, there is a path on the right, down some steps and through an underpass which leads into Mollie Quirk's Glen.

One can climb up to the main road and turn left for the bus stop (service to Douglas or Laxey), or retrace one's steps to the car park by Port Groudle.

Groudle Helen

13. Port Soderick Glen

OS Map ref. start: 346727
Terrain: Easy
Access: Take the Old Castletown Road (A25) from Douglas, turn left down a minor road (B23) signed Port Soderick. At the end of the road there is parking by the entrance to the glen. There is an infrequent bus service timed with start and finish of the school day.

The path through woodland populated with spring flowers follows the course of the Crogga River. The river enters the sea at a scenic bay.

This is a delightful glen, in particular in spring and early summer when the daffodils, bluebells and wild garlic contribute their colours and scents to the walk. It was adopted by the Government as a National Glen in 1975. On entering the glen take the right path, which is well maintained, keeping the Crogga River on your left. Pass open areas which used to, and can still, become a little boggy. In the past cars that parked here would occasionally become trapped and the local farmer would pull them out with his tractor for a fee of £25!

Towards the end the path rises towards wooden fencing, here one can take a brief diversion by following the steps uphill on the right. The path curves right and flattens giving you views of the glen from high up. This path eventually takes you out of the glen, so walk a few hundred yards further to appreciate the view before heading back.

Re-join the main path and head downstream. Cross the bridge so now the river is on the left. The path climbs a little way into the woodland before dropping down to the riverbank. Follow this path past the main bridge and ascend a short flight of stone steps. Pass through the gate and follow the concrete track to the bay.

Port Soderick. This was a thriving destination for holidaymakers in late 19th and early 20th centuries. It offered refreshment rooms, side show stalls, an amusement arcade and boating: candles were sold to explore the caves (to the right as one looks out to sea). The large building formerly housed an amusement arcade and paddling pool. There was a cliff top tramway from Douglas Head which transported visitors in their hundreds each day during the summer. To reach the beach there was a funicular railway (now removed). On the pillar by a flight of steps leading to the breakwater one can see a plaque which references the Forrester brothers, the entrepreneurs who established these facilities in 1897.

Crogga River

14. Silverdale Glen

OS Map ref. start: 275710
Terrain: Easy
Access: At Ballasalla roundabout (on A5) head north signed A26 St Marks and Foxdale. Straight over the next roundabout and in a few hundred yards take a left turn and another left turn signed Silverdale. Just over a small bridge there is a car park by the café. (If this is busy follow signs to additional car park but return to this one to start the walk). Ballasalla has a frequent bus service and Manx Electric Railway station.

A woodland walk by a stream which feeds into an ornamental pond, there is an historic merry-go-round. The glen extends southwards passing an historic pack-horse bridge. Rushen Abbey is located at the southern end of the walk.

Silverdale Glen. The centre of the glen has a café, boating lake and a children's playground including a magnificent water-powered roundabout. The latter was constructed in about 1890 and is the only surviving and working one in Europe to be driven by water. There is a large grassed area which allows space for games and picnicking. It was established as a recreational area for summer visitors in the late 19th century. At the end of the pond is a white building which used to be the Silverburn Glen Mineral Water factory. The Cregg Mill by the bridge was built in 1760s to process flax. The boating lake was originally the dam providing water for the wheel in the mill.

There are two walks from here.

The shorter walk is to take the path round the pond, pass the uphill path on the left (which takes one to a car park) and carry on forwards. Follow the path with the Silverburn River on the left, pass the bridge on the right. Cross over the small metal bridge where the river bifurcates, with the small stream going through the sluice gate. The path narrows a little as one heads upstream and ends at the main road.

Return by the same route, this time cross over the wooden bridge and right down the steps. In a few hundred yards there is a bridge which takes one across a grassy picnic area to the playground. Return to the car park.

For the second walk proceed up the road away from the café for 20 yards until a wooden fence by an information board on the left is reached: this is the entrance to the lower glen. After a few yards take the path which hairpins left down towards the stream. There is a plaque commemorating when the glen was given over by the Quine family to the Manx National Trust. Continue down the path through the woods favouring the slightly higher track. There is a weir with a narrow channel.

Follow the higher path which has a couple of concrete steps. This slopes gently downhill to pass the Monk's Well on the right – the monks being from nearby Rushen Abbey. Continue by taking a brief detour over the bridge to see the mill pond which is usually a home to ducks. Return to the path which passes through a pair of low gateposts with 'Silverdale Glen' and 'Grey Tower' on them (the name of a large house on Silverdale Road), and bear left.

On the right, obscured by bushes, there are the remains of what was probably a lime kiln. Kilns were used to heat limestone to high temperatures to convert it to quicklime: slaked lime (calcium hydroxide) would be formed by mixing it with water, this would be used as a fertiliser on farmland. Limestone was quarried at Scarlett, just south of Castletown, until 1930s.

The glen walk ends at the pack-horse bridge. It is called the Monks' Bridge and is also known as *Crossag*, in Manx this means 'Little crossing'. The bridge was built in 1350 by the Cistercian monks of nearby Rushen Abbey and it allowed the monks to pass over the Silverburn River to travel to their farms in the north (also to give access to the Abbot's gallows which were situated about a mile north at Black Hill). It is believed to be the best preserved medieval bridge in the British Isles.

Continue along this road with the river on your left until it ends in a ford. In front is the Abbey Restaurant and on the left of the car park a path leads to the entrance of Rushen Abbey.

Rushen Abbey. This Cistercian abbey was established in 1134 on lands granted to the Abbot of Furness (Lancashire) by the Viking King Olaf who ruled the Isle of Man. This location was chosen as it was close to Castletown where the King had settled, so he could keep an eye on what the monks were doing. The Abbey was granted certain rights and privileges: it rose to become one of the most powerful institutions on the Island owning large tracts of land. After Henry VIII dissolved the monasteries in 1540s much of

The Monk's Well

the Abbey was plundered for building stone, hence the ruins that we see today. There is a comprehensive exhibition outlining what life might have been like in the Abbey, and a walk around the remains of the Abbey building (admission charge).

Retrace one's steps the glen car park or continue past the Abbey to the main road and turn left for Ballasalla.

Silverdale Glen

Glen Maye

15. Glen Maye

OS Map ref. start: 236798
Terrain: Easy, occasionally moderately steep
Access: Glen Maye is on A27 about 5 miles south of Peel, there is a car park by the Waterfall Inn (closed). There is an occasional bus service

A spectacular and profusely vegetated gorge which extends down to the sea, a dramatic waterfall with an excellent viewing platform.

Glen Maye. The glen was once known as 'Glen Mea' - the 'Luxuriant Glen'. The glen used to be owned by the Waterfall Inn which charged a 3d entrance fee: it was acquired by the Forestry Board in 1960. The sheltered fern-filled woodland includes relics of the ancient forests that once covered the Isle of Man. There is an abundance of large ferns which thrive in the mild, sheltered climate. In the middle of the glen are remains of a building that used to house a waterwheel which pumped water out of a small mine that was operational from 1740s until 1870s (known as 'The Mona Erin').

The entrance to the glen is at the bottom of the car park down a flight of steps: there are public toilets on the right. The sound of rushing water is soon apparent as the river throws itself down narrow channels and over the rocks. The waterfall (*Spooty Vooar*) is said to be the home of the mythical Buggane. Pause on the bridge over the river to look at the waterfall and downstream towards the steep cliffs which can hide the glen completely from sunlight.

The Buggane. In Manx folklore the Buggane is a mischief maker invariably depicted as a hairy, often ugly creature – akin to the Scandinavian troll. It can appear in any shape it pleases – as an ogre with a huge head and great fiery eyes; as a small dog which grows larger and larger as you watch it; as horned monster or anything it chooses. Each Buggane has his own particular dwelling-place, but hiding behind waterfalls is particularly favoured.

Use the path that closely follows the course of the river, the return will be by the higher level route (the turnings on the left). The path becomes easier to walk, and some stretches are concreted. The damp microclimate enables a variety of ferns and other plants to flourish. After a while the river widens and runs more gently. The path briefly goes uphill by a flight of steps but climbs down to follow the river. A bridge crosses the river so it is now on the left.

On the right are the remains of the building that used to house a waterwheel which pumped water out of the small mine. Walking round and peering through the archway helps one appreciate how long, narrow and tall the building was in order to house the waterwheel.

A gate leads onto a minor road which heads downhill – now there is an aerial view of the wheelhouse. Passing over a footbridge the sea comes into view and cliffs now tower above. Follow the path down to the shingle beach. The coves around here are said to have been used for smuggling in the 17th century.

Return the same way back to the gate that leads into the glen then back over the bridge. This time follow the upper path which affords a different view of the river as it is now 50–60 feet below. The path is wide, flat and easy to negotiate and eventually returns one to the first bridge that was crossed to enter the glen.

16. Colby Glen

OS Map ref. start: 231710
Terrain: Easy
Access: Follow A7 from Ballasalla through Ballabeg, take a right turn (Colby Glen Road, A27) a couple of hundred yards past Colby Glen Hotel . Follow the road uphill for half a mile to the lower entrance. Colby is served by buses and the Steam Railway.

A tranquil wooded glen following the river, leads to a countryside walk to a small hamlet.

Colby Glen. The glen was purchased by the Government from private ownership in 1955 for £50. Apart from clearing the paths and bridges it is one of the few glens that is not actively managed but left to nature. The land had been owned privately for generations but locals had walked through the glens unchallenged. Then, for a reason not recorded, the owners decided to erect gates to prevent access in 1912. Crowds of locals assembled and took the law into their hands to re-instate their right of way and smashed down the gates. Police were powerless to intervene as the subject of public access to the area was ambiguous.

Proceed through the gate and down steps and across a bridge to join a path by the river. As one walks up the glen two series of steps take the path above the river and then down again. There is a section where the river has cut a deep gorge and there is evidence of storm damage with a tree trunk lying across the river.

At the top of the glen there is a flat area with picnic benches and an 'insect hotel'. Just by a footpath sign bear left and right before a flight of steps. This area can be muddy following wet weather, the path leads to a series of small river cascades. Return towards the bridge by the flat area. There are now three walking options. Either cross the bridge and take the steps in front which lead to the upper entrance where the road can be followed back to the lower entrance. Or retrace one's steps back along the glen to the lower entrance

Alternatively, one can add a short country walk to Ballakilpheric (about a mile away) by following the footpath sign and climbing the flight of steps with the handrail. After a short climb the path levels off with the hedgerows replete with bluebells in the spring. After a moderate climb go through the metal kissing-gate the path continues through open countryside with views over Castletown, Langness and Ronaldsway Airport.

At an old wooden gate the path turns left and soon left again to reach Ballakilpheric – a notable feature of the village is the Victorian Methodist chapel. Ballakilpheric is the anglicised version of the Manx *Balley keeill Pharick* which translates as '*the farm of Patrick's church*' – the little church is no longer there. Return by the same path, remembering to turn right through the old gate.

Colby Glen

17. Bradda Glen

OS Map ref. **start:** 195697
Terrain: Easy
Access: Take the main road (A32) through Port Erin, round the top of the bay and uphill. There is on-street parking near the entrance to Bradda Glen. Port Erin is served by buses and the Steam Railway.

Initially a wooded walk, the route then follows cliff-top paths with views across Port Erin Bay and the cliff coastline southwards.

Proceed through the Bradda Glen archway (made from local slate) following the sloping path: after a minute there is a sharp left turn which takes one back to the town. Continue straight on past this on the main path towards the café. (There is another path on the left which gives the option of visiting the rocky shore).

Past the café take the higher surfaced path on the left to commence a return loop around the cliff-top. Soon there is a viewing platform overlooking the bay and information boards on the birds, fish and sea mammals that it is possible to see. To the left on the rocks it is possible to make out the remains of an open-air salt water swimming pool which operated from 1910s to 1970s. Proceed forwards across the grassed area to a concrete path which goes round the base of Bradda Head with views across the Irish Sea. To the edge of the cliff on the left one can make out a tower which is the remains of engine house used to pump water out of the Bradda

Mines – commercial mining was carried out in 18th and 19th centuries.

Milner's Tower. This was built in 1871 atop Bradda Head as a tribute to William Milner who earned his wealth as a maker of fire-resistant safes in Liverpool. In the later part of his life he lived in Port Erin and was a great benefactor to the town. The funds for the tower were raised by public donations and the design of the tower is said to represent the shape of the key to his very first safe. The tower was meant to be built in secret (how could that be achieved when it is in such a prominent position?). However, when Milner found out he donated much of the building cost himself.

At the sign 'Bradda Head Nature Trail 10' there is the option of heading up to Bradda Head. To return to the glen by the lower route take the path on the left. This gives closer views of the rocky shore: this is clearly a much loved walk judging by the number of benches with memorial plaques. Return past the café and up to the glen entrance.

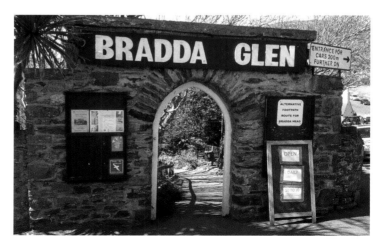

View from Bradda Glen looking towards Port Erin

CONTENTS

		Page
Introduction		
	1. The High Hills of Teesdale	4
	2. Access & the Right to Roam	6
	3. The Walks	8
	4. The Weather	9
	5. The Maps	9
	6. Towns, Villages & Accommodation	10
	7. Tourist Information Centres & Websites	10
Walk 1: Bink Moss		15
Walk 2: Fendrith Hill		23
Walk 3: James Hill		30
Walk 4: Meldon Hill		38
Walk 5: Viewing Hill		46
Walk 6: Three Pikes and Great Stony Hill		53
Walk 7: Burnhope Seat		62
Walk 8: Mickle Fell		68
Moor House Nature Reserve		75
Appendix		
	Using the route diagrams	76
	Ferguson Grading System	76
	The Author	80
	Trailguides Limited	81
	Acknowledgements	82
	Disclaimer	82

INTRODUCTION

1.   The High Hills of Teesdale

Teesdale, one of the most popular walking areas in the North East and extolled by Wainwright in his book on the Pennine Way for its "sylvan beauty". However there is another side to this picturesque dale and that is of the high moorland peaks that surround it.

As the river Tees makes its way down from its birthplace on the slopes of Cross Fell it passes eight distinct hills each soaring above the two thousand foot mark that qualifies them as a mountain. Totally different from the usual image of the Lakeland mountain, these are a ring of moorland summits clad in heather and peat instead of rock. These hills may not have the height and the grandeur of the Lakes peaks but in their own way they can be just as challenging and rewarding to walk.

You wouldn't find the crowds of peak-baggers on these hills, these are built for solitude and isolation. Here you will be unlucky if you come across another walker. Just yourself, the grouse and the curlew, the hill walker's dream ....

Looking back towards High Cup as you climb towards Meldon.
Walk 4. Meldon Hill.

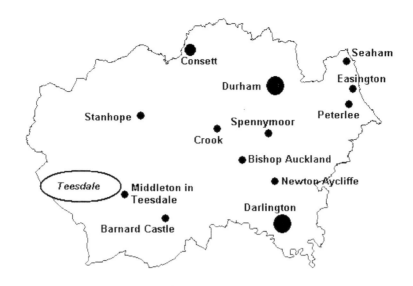

In the world of the peak-bagger, those walkers who set out to climb the high hills and then tick them off a list, these hills of Teesdale are classified as HEWITT's, Hills in England, Wales and Ireland over Two Thousand feet. The classification being a hill over two thousand feet (610 metres) with a drop of at least 98 feet (30 metres) on each side.

There are 525 HEWITT's in total, 177 in England, 137 in Wales and 211 in Ireland. On the high moorland surrounding Teesdale there are eight summits falling into this HEWITT classification.

Mickle Fell	2,585 ft/788 metres
Meldon Hill	2,516 ft/767 metres
Burnhope Seat	2,450 ft/747 metres
Great Stony Hill	2,323 ft/708 metres
James Hill	2,215 ft/675 metres
Three Pikes	2,136 ft/651 metres
Viewing Hill	2,129 ft/649 metres
Bink Moss	2,031 ft/619 metres
Fendrith Hill	2,283 ft/696 metres

Fendrith Hill is an outlying hill of the Chapelfell Top summit of Weardale and therefore does not qualify as a HEWITT however it is a nice hill to walk and completes the round of these high Teesdale hills.

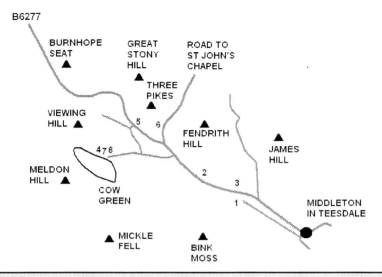

B6277

BURNHOPE
SEAT
▲

GREAT
STONY
HILL
▲

ROAD TO
ST JOHN'S
CHAPEL
▲

THREE
PIKES
▲

VIEWING
HILL ▲

5   6

FENDRITH
HILL
▲

JAMES
HILL
▲

4 7 8

2

3

MELDON
HILL ▲

COW
GREEN

1

MIDDLETON
IN TEESDALE
●

▲ MICKLE
FELL

▲
BINK
MOSS

The High Hills of Teesdale and the start of the walks.

2. Access & the Right to Roam

None of the hills of Teesdale have a right of way that crosses their summit. Technically this made them out of bounds for the hill walker although in practice, being the friendly folk that they are, as long as you were keeping to the high ground and not causing any damage then a blind eye was normally turned by the farmers and tenants of the dale.

With the implementation of the Countryside Right of Way Act 2000 in 2005 and the "Right to Roam" this has now changed and all the upland areas of Teesdale have now become legally accessible with the exception of Mickle Fell which stands on Ministry of Defence land and has it's own rules and regulations but more on that one later.

This legislation allows walkers the right to roam at will over "designated access land" without the need to be restricted to official footpaths and bridleways. On the new editions of the Ordnance Survey Explorer maps, this new access land is marked with a light yellow coloured background and at the entry points to this land, the stiles and gates carry the new "access land" waymarking symbol of a brown stick man in a brown circle.

With the right to access has also come responsibility and the walker is expected to observe various limits and restrictions that are placed on their activities at certain times of the year. The landowner and/or farmer has the right to exclude access for up to twenty eight days per year and this normally applies between May and early July and coincides with the breeding season of the ground-nesting birds on the moors. Where they are known any restrictions that may impinge on the given walk are shown in the details for that walk. However, don't take it for granted that these are going to be accurate. Every year circumstances can and do change and restrictions may alter, always check any notices that are placed at the access points for any restrictions. Further information on both access and general and specific restrictions can be found on the website **www.countrysideaccess.gov.uk**

For those that walk with their dogs, access land does still have some restrictions. Large parts of Upper Teesdale are part of the Moor House National Nature Reserve and so for conservation reasons, dogs may be excluded from these areas. In those areas where they are permitted, as with all walking, there is the requirement to keep your dog under close control and under the CRoW Act that is stipulated as being on a lead.

By using the right to roam and moving away from the recognised foot-

Rough going across the peat hags. Walk 1. Bink Moss.

paths and bridleways, the walker does become more exposed to potential hazards. As with most parts of the North Pennines, Teesdale has been heavily exploited in the past for its mineral wealth. This has left a legacy of old workings, quarries and shafts all of which can be hazardous. Caution must always be exercised when in the vicinity of any of these sites.

The highest of the Teesdale hills, Mickle Fell, lies on Ministry of Defence land and forms part of the over-shoot area of the Warcop ranges. For safety reasons access to this area is normally prohibited but on certain days of the year the land is opened up to the public giving the walker a chance to visit the summit of the fell. Normally the access dates are published a year in advance and can be obtained via the MOD website at
www.defence-estates.mod.uk
or by contacting the following office.
DE Operations North—Land Management Services (North)
Defence Training Estate North, Warcop Training Area, Warcop,
Appleby-in-Westmorland, Cumbria, CA16 6PA.
Telephone 01768 343227

For safety reasons walkers are restricted to pre-defined routes when visiting Mickle Fell and an access permit has to be obtained from the above MOD estate office. Applying for the permit is relatively easy but does involve returning a signed safety brief so it would be advisable to give yourself a couple of weeks notice before your walk. Don't let the bureaucracy put you off what is a very good walk and, anyway, the staff at the MOD estate office are very helpful and friendly. When making enquiries and applying for the visit to Mickle Fell the route that you will be using will be the Mickle Fell Access Permit North from Teesdale.

3. The Walks

The walks in this book are not for the inexperienced. They traverse the nine highest hills that nestle in the wild moorland that surrounds the valley of Teesdale. This countryside is wild, exposed and pathless. The sole purpose of these walks is to provide a route so that the walker can say "yes, I've been up that hill". However, saying that, all of these walks are within the capability of the reasonably fit and competent hill walker who has a basic knowledge of using a map and compass.

The walks have all been graded in accordance with the Ferguson Grading System ('FGS') and the actual grading is set out at the beginning of each individual walk. A detailed explanation of the FGS and how individual gradings are determined is set out on pages 76-79 in the Appendix to this book

The walks in this book may not be the best or even the easiest routes up this collection of hills. I'm sure that somebody out there will have a different approach to each and every one of them. However, this is my choice and, in the main, I've enjoyed each of the challenges that these hills have presented.

Teesdale may be a popular walking area but once you get away from the well-trodden paths in the valley floor, the isolation and the solitude will surprise you. With the exception of Mickle Fell on none of these walks did we encounter another soul once we had started on the slopes. The High Hills of Teesdale may not have the glamour and stark ruggedness of the Lakes but these moorland mountains deserve to be visited for what they are, a pool of quiet contemplation in an over-crowded sea of congestion.

4. The Weather

The weather in the North Pennines can be very changeable even during summer. The exposed altitude of this part of County Durham can make even a balmy summer's day seem cold and uninviting. When you are near the top of one of these high hills, mist and low cloud can be experienced at any time of the year and can roll in quite quickly catching the walker unaware. Don't misjudge this high country, although due to global warming the heavy snow falls of yesteryear aren't so regular now but they do still happen. When walking at any time of the year be prepared and equipped for all weather conditions.

5. The Maps

Two maps cover the high hills of Teesdale.
Ordinance Survey Explorer OL31 North Pennines Teesdale & Weardale.
Ordinance Survey Explorer OL19 Howgill Fells & Upper Eden Valley.

The relevant map will be shown in the details of the individual walk. On a couple of the walks both maps will be required.

The route diagrams included in this book are meant as a guide, they are not intended to replace the use of the relevant map. It would be foolhardy to venture onto these hills with just this guidebook and no map.

6. Towns, Villages & Accommodation

The small town of Middleton in Teesdale is the focal point of Upper Teesdale and makes the perfect base for exploring the dale. There is a choice of accommodation ranging from small hotels, guest·houses, self catering cottages and caravan/camping sites within the dale although most shops and facilities are within Middleton. In addition there is the youth hostel at Langden Beck and bookings can be made on-line at www.yha.org.uk or by calling 0870 770 5910. The Tourist Information Centres in Middleton in Teesdale and Barnard Castle, see below, will be happy to assist with any specific requirements.

7. Tourist Information Centres & Websites

The Upper Teesdale valley falls within the North Pennines Area of out-standing natural beauty. Although the AONB does not operate a visitor centre in Teesdale they do operate a very useful website giving information on the flora, fauna, geology, attractions and events of the North Pennines. The website can be found at
www.northpennines.org.uk

Within Teesdale there are two Tourist Information Centres, one situated in the upper part of the dale in Middleton in Teesdale and the other further down the valley in Barnard Castle. Contact details of both are below.

Middleton in Teesdale Tourist Information Centre, 10 Market Place, Middleton in Teesdale, County Durham DL12 0QG
Phone. 01833 641001
Open seven days a week throughout the year between 10 am and 1 pm.

Barnard Castle Tourist Information Centre, Woodleigh, Flatts Road, Barnard Castle, County Durham DL12 8AA
Phone: 01833 690909

In addition to the TIC's there are a number of websites that can supply further information about the dale and the facilities available. A small selection are listed below.
www.teesdale.gov.uk
www.teesdalediscovery.com
www.teesdaleholidays.co.uk
www.teesdale.co.uk

Above. The barely discernable summit as indicated by the old pole sticking out of the peat. Walk 1. Bink Moss.
Below. The summit trig point with a distant Cow Green reservoir and Meldon Hill in the background. Walk 2. Fendrith Hill.

Above. Bog-hopping on the way to the trig point. Walk 3. James Hill.
Below. The remains of the summit trig point. Walk 4. Meldon Hill.

12

Above. The summit plateau of Viewing Hill with Three Pikes and Great Stony Hill in the background. Walk 5. Viewing Hill.
Below. Three Pikes summit cairn with Cow Green reservoir in the background. Walk 6. Three Pikes and Great Stony Hill.

13

Above. Great Dun Fell, Little Dun Fell and Cross Fell from the old miner's track alongside Cow Green. Walk 7. Burnhope Seat. Below. The exceptionally large summit cairn. Walk 8. Mickle Fell.

WALK 1: BINK MOSS

The name Moss says it all. The summit of this hill encompasses a wide bleak moorland plateau of rough grass and peat bog with not even a trig point to it's name. The fact that a wire fence runs close to the summit is the only thing that makes the top easy to locate. There is an old pole stuck in the mud to indicate the position of the high point but for all of the point's distinctiveness it could just as well be ten or fifteen feet either side and you would never be able to tell. There's even a peat hag to negotiate within the last couple of feet in order to get to the summit pole itself.

However after saying that this is a true wild walk and on a day with good visibility there are some grand views over the remote uplands of upper Teesdale. This is a walk where you would be very lucky (or unlucky !) to meet anybody else. Be prepared to rough it, the going is hard and you will definitely get your feet wet as there are a number of streams to jump, ford or simply just wade across, some of them quite deep and fast flowing. On a bad day this walk can be very exposed.

They talk about the North Pennines being "England's Last Wilderness" and on this walk you can really believe it

DISTANCE: 8.6 mile (13.8 km)
ASCENT: 1,250 feet (381 metres)
TERRAIN: Open fell with large sections of peat hags and gullies. The route does return to Holwick along a good quality vehicle track. There are a number of streams to be crossed on this route which in bad weather may present some difficulties.
TIME: 4 to 5 hours.
START: Small car parking space alongside the head of the road through Holwick. GR NY 904 270.
MAP: OL31 North Pennines Teesdale and Weardale.
　　　　OL19 Howgill Fells & Upper Eden Valley.
DOGS: The initial climb up through Holwick crags may give a problem but after that should be ok. Sheep will be encountered throughout the route.
ACCESS: The majority of this walk is on open access land.

Grid References

Holwick	904 270
Bridleway junction	901 271
Gate	904 246

Bink Moss	875 243
Hagworm Hill	865 244
Stream	864 256
Path/track junction	862 270
Sheep stile	899 272
Holwick	904 270

FGS Grading

Grading is F10 [D1, N2, T3, R2, H2]

Distance	1	6 – 12 miles
Navigation	2	Competent navigation skills needed
Terrain	3	Under 25% on graded track or path Over 75% off track
Remoteness	2	Countryside not in close proximity to habitation – less than 20% of the route within 2 miles
Height	2	Over 125 ft per mile

Start : Parking space at the head of the road through Holwick. GR 904 270.

From the parking space go through the gate and past the solitary house standing alongside the track. Follow the main track as it heads uphill to go between the two sets of crags as shown below. After the track reaches the top of the rise it starts a shallow descent and here a wooden post marks where a bridleway leaves the track on the left and goes steeply downhill to cross the stream. Follow the bridleway down, across the stream and up the steep climb through the crags on the other side.

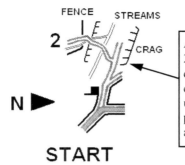

FENCE STREAMS

2

CRAG

N ▶

START

At the bridleway sign, GR 901 271, turn left and descend steeply down to the stream, cross and then climb steeply up the other side and up through the crags and follow the path through the gate and alongside the stream.

├──────────────────┤
1 KM APPROX.

Climbing up through the crags after crossing the stream.

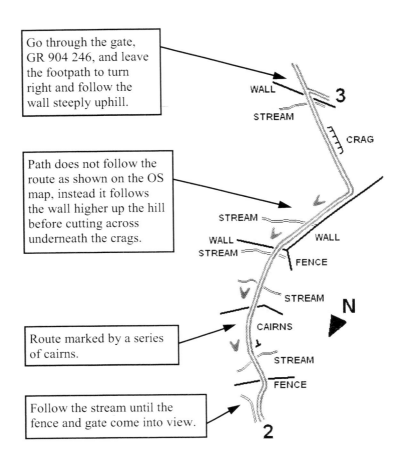

Go through the gate, GR 904 246, and leave the footpath to turn right and follow the wall steeply uphill.

WALL

STREAM

3

CRAG

Path does not follow the route as shown on the OS map, instead it follows the wall higher up the hill before cutting across underneath the crags.

STREAM

WALL

STREAM

WALL

FENCE

STREAM

N

Route marked by a series of cairns.

CAIRNS

STREAM

FENCE

Follow the stream until the fence and gate come into view.

2

Walking alongside the stream after Holwick Crags.

18

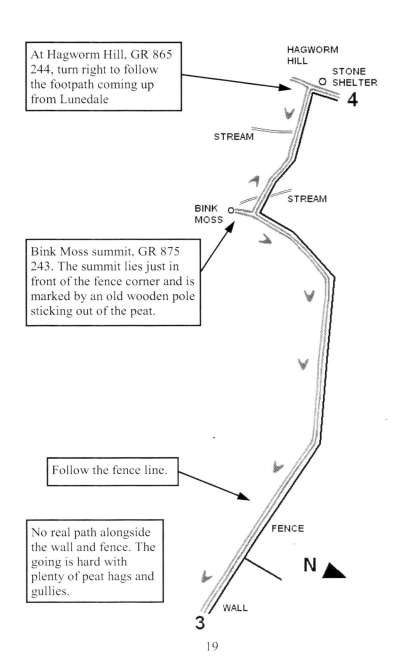

At Hagworm Hill, GR 865 244, turn right to follow the footpath coming up from Lunedale

HAGWORM HILL

STONE
O SHELTER

4

STREAM

STREAM

BINK O
MOSS

Bink Moss summit, GR 875 243. The summit lies just in front of the fence corner and is marked by an old wooden pole sticking out of the peat.

Follow the fence line.

FENCE

No real path alongside the wall and fence. The going is hard with plenty of peat hags and gullies.

N

WALL

3

19

GR 862 270, the path crosses a well-surfaced vehicle track but instead of going straight across turn right to follow the track.

Path becomes non-existent. Follow the marker posts.

GR 864 256, the path crosses a stream and then heads away from the fence line following a series of marker posts that indicate the route of the path.

Below. Following the fence line as it descends from Hagworm Hill.

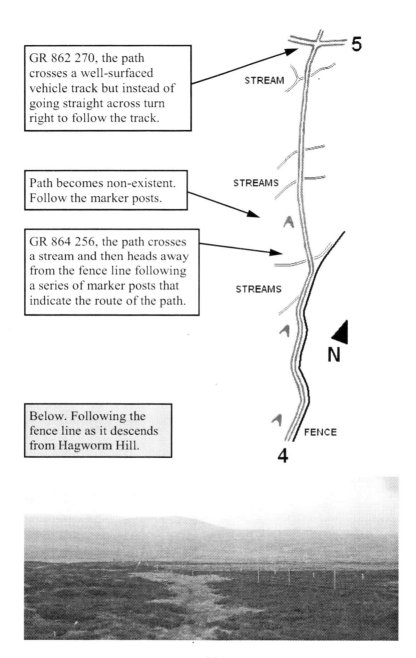

STREAM

STREAMS

STREAMS

N

FENCE

5

4

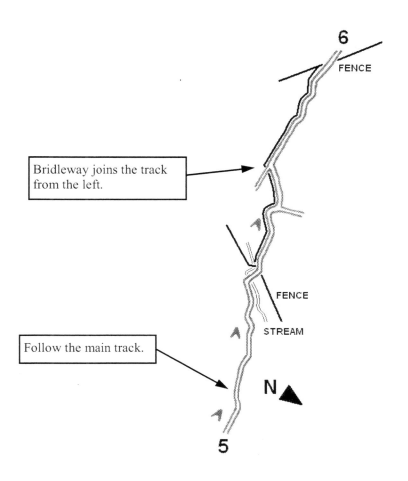

6

FENCE

Bridleway joins the track from the left.

FENCE

STREAM

Follow the main track.

N

5

FINISH

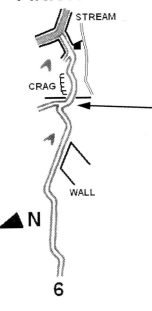

STREAM

CRAG

WALL

▲N

6

GR 899 272, the main track bears left and heads downhill, leave the main track and go straight ahead over the stone sheep stile. See photo below.

The author in his younger days running down the main track and past the sheep stile.

WALK 2: FENDRITH HILL

At 2,283 feet (696 metres), Fendrith Hill is not the smallest hill in this book but it is the only one that does not qualify as a HEWITT. It is in fact an outlying hill of the Chapelfell Top summit, the top of that hill lying in Weardale and so outside the scope of this book although it will be visited in the High Hills of Weardale. From the Teesdale side this is the nearest hilltop to Chapelfell.

Fendrith has a charm of its own and is relatively easily accessible from the Hanging Shaw car park. The summit of the hill is marked with its own trig point from which there are good views across Cow Green reservoir to the Cross Fell range and in the opposite direction down the Teesdale valley itself.

On the route you pass close enough to have a quick look at the only cave system in the dale located at High Hurth Edge. At first glance these look like no more than small cracks in the face of the crag. However the crags can be followed round and through a gate where the entrances become larger and are capable of being pot-holed. Not that you'd get me into them, my family spent far too many generations trying to get out of the pits just to have me start going back underground as a hobby.

Its not just us humans that have used these caves as within them the bones of lynx have been discovered. This large cat was a native of these dales in prehistoric times but became extinct in this country long before the Roman invasion, probably dying out between 10,000 BC and AD43.

Further up the track the route curves it's way round the site of Church Bowers Quarry which is the home of the walls and roofs of most of the older houses in the dale. The first sighting of it is three large stone cairns sitting on a long mound of stones. Marked on the map as a single cairn these are very prominent and can be seen from various points around the route. Sadly, according to the map, these three ladies have no name which is somewhat of a shame for such large well-constructed cairns. My walking companion suggested Hubble-Bubble, Toil and Trouble. Anyone better that ?

The quarry itself is a bit of an oddity. Normally you'd expect a quarry to be a big hole in the ground with rock faces from where the stone was extracted, instead this one seems to have more above ground than below it, in fact it is more a mound of stone than a hole. The surprising thing is that, as the track makes it's way round the outside of the quarry there appears to be passage-ways cut into the mound. Most of these passage-ways have a walled lining so that they are obviously deliberate constructions leading into the interior of the mound. The question is why and for what reason ??

Potential Hazard.
When you leave the road at Swinhope Head the footpath sign indicating the direction of the path is at the wrong angle and points you in the direction of a hut on the skyline on the opposite ridge. This hut is not marked on the map and is not the shooting hut that you should be heading for at GR 887 316. At this point the correct hut is not visible as it lies behind the ridge line. Following a straight line to the wrong hut will take you through an extensive area of old mine shafts and workings.

To follow the correct route you need to stay high and contour round the head of the small valley until you reach the opposite ridge and from there locate the shooting hut. Hasten to add that the footpath that you are following may be shown on the map but does not exist on the ground which is why it is so easy to go wrong on this stretch.

DISTANCE: 8.3 mile (13.3 km)
ASCENT: 1,480 feet (451 metres)
TERRAIN: Initially gravel track giving way to grass track before becoming a walk over pathless moor. The route finishes with a short road section leading back on to the initial gravel track.
TIME: 4 to 5 hours.
START: Hanging Shaw car park. GR NY 867 298
MAP: OL31 North Pennines Teesdale and Weardale.
DOGS: No obstacles such as stiles to contend with but there is one fence to climb over however the route does pass through a couple of farms where you may meet other dogs and there is a short section on quiet, isolated road. Sheep will be encountered throughout the route and so will cattle in a couple of the lower fields.
ACCESS: The initial outward leg up the side of the valley and the return from Swinhope Head are on public rights of way. The majority of the route is on public access land.

Grid References

Hanging Shaw Car park	867 298
Gate	870 312
End of track	871 327
Fendrith Hill	877 333

Swinhope Head	898 332
Shooting hut	887 316
Road junction	882 299
Track crossroads	869 309
Hanging Shaw Car park	867 298

FGS Grading

Grading is F9 [D1, N2, T2, R2, H2]

Distance	1	6 – 12 miles
Navigation	2	Competent navigation skills needed
Terrain	2	25 -50% on graded track or path 50 – 75% off track
Remoteness	2	Countryside not in close proximity to habitation – less than 20% of the route within 2 miles
Height	2	Over 125 ft per mile

Start : Hanging Shaw car park. GR 867 298.

From the car park head up the lane indicated by the footpath sign and follow the obvious main track as it heads uphill. See photo below.

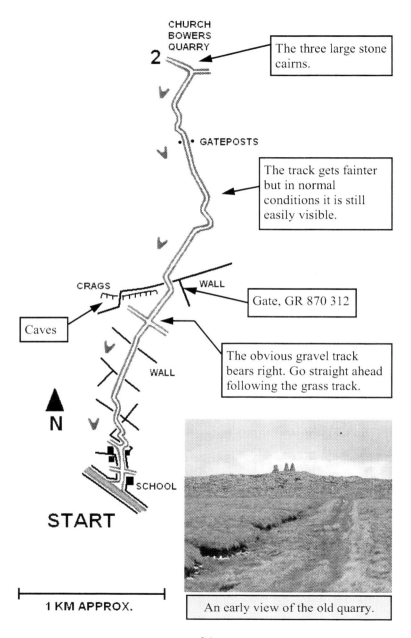

CHURCH
BOWERS
QUARRY

2

The three large stone cairns.

GATEPOSTS

The track gets fainter but in normal conditions it is still easily visible.

CRAGS

WALL

Gate, GR 870 312

Caves

The obvious gravel track bears right. Go straight ahead following the grass track.

WALL

N

SCHOOL

START

1 KM APPROX.

An early view of the old quarry.

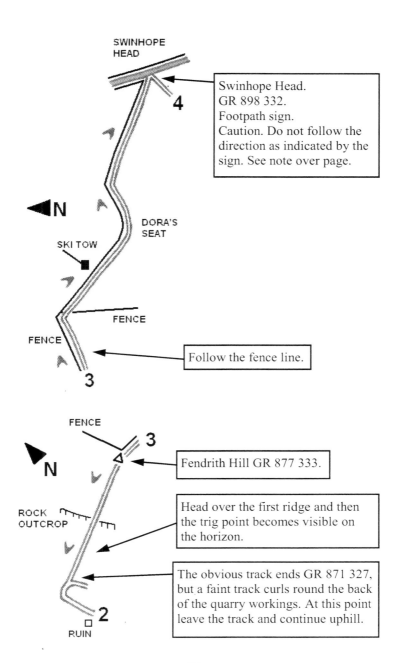

SWINHOPE
HEAD

Swinhope Head.
GR 898 332.
Footpath sign.
Caution. Do not follow the
direction as indicated by the
sign. See note over page.

4

◀N

DORA'S
SEAT

SKI TOW

FENCE

FENCE

Follow the fence line.

3

FENCE

3

▲N

Fendrith Hill GR 877 333.

ROCK
OUTCROP

Head over the first ridge and then
the trig point becomes visible on
the horizon.

The obvious track ends GR 871 327,
but a faint track curls round the back
of the quarry workings. At this point
leave the track and continue uphill.

2

RUIN

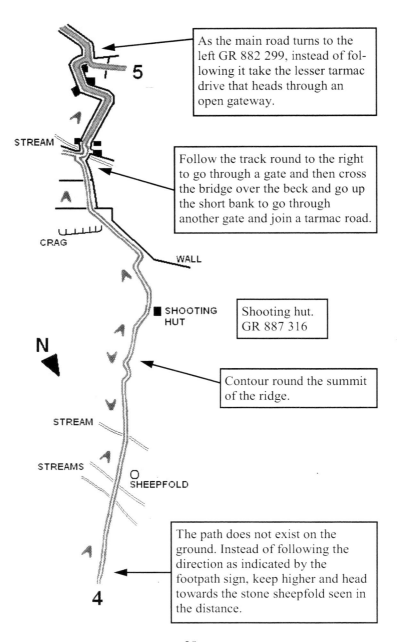

As the main road turns to the left GR 882 299, instead of following it take the lesser tarmac drive that heads through an open gateway.

5

STREAM

Follow the track round to the right to go through a gate and then cross the bridge over the beck and go up the short bank to go through another gate and join a tarmac road.

CRAG

WALL

■ SHOOTING HUT

Shooting hut.
GR 887 316

N

Contour round the summit of the ridge.

STREAM

STREAMS

O SHEEPFOLD

The path does not exist on the ground. Instead of following the direction as indicated by the footpath sign, keep higher and head towards the stone sheepfold seen in the distance.

4

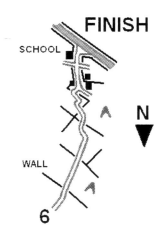

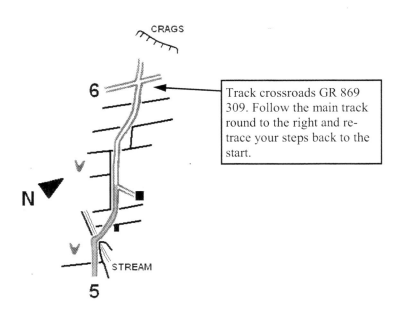

Track crossroads GR 869 309. Follow the main track round to the right and re-trace your steps back to the start.

WALK 3: JAMES HILL

The most easterly of the big hills of Teesdale and one that is well worth the visit if not for the summit then to view the 4,000 year old site lying on the flanks of this hill.

The summit of James Hill is relatively easy to find as it lies on the watershed between Teesdale and Weardale. Following the boundary fence brings you to the trig point marking the spot. Like most of the Teesdale tops the trig pillar stands in the midst of a peaty mess but in this case there is a very boggy quad track going past the trig which is utilised for the homeward leg. Don't expect spectacular views from this hilltop, the summit plateau is very wide and prevents any good views.

Carr Crags Cup Marked Stones

Located on the flank of James Hill is a wide area of stones and boulders known as Carr Crags. At the western end of this outcropping lies a group of over thirty rocks that are unique in the North East and possibly the country. Grouped around a massive central stone block these boulders form a rough keyhole shape across the slope of the hill.

Carved and ground into the surface of these stones including the central block, are over three hundred cup marks which range in size from five inches across to much larger "basin" sized markings. To the uninitiated a cup mark is a circular depression that has been deliberately carved and ground into the surface of a rock during prehistoric times. As with the

Stood on top of the central stone with a couple of the larger cup marked stones in front.

stones at this site, they can even be laid out in a pattern that can cover the whole or a section of rock. Cup-marks can range from simple hollows about five inches across to much larger "basin" shapes. These markings may be found singularly or in groups and are collectively known as rock art.

The age of the carvings at Carr Crags is not known but the use of this rock art is believed to span the two thousand years between 4,000 BC and 2,000 BC. This period is known as the Neolithic or New Stone Age and at this time the landscape would have been very different from today with lightly forested uplands overlooking the more fertile, richer and densely-forested river valleys. It is at this point in time that our ancestors were making the slow change from the hunter/gatherer style of civilisation to that of the pasturalist through the development of husbandry and agriculture. For a long period both these cultures co-existed and quite often this rock art is found in areas where the limits of the hunter/gatherer and the pasturalist met and crossed.

Rock art is formed from various sized depressions in the rock and may be accompanied by surrounding concentric rings and also by grooves that

A pattern of the larger "basin" markings.

may link the cup marks together. The reasons for these stone markings are unknown however various suggestions have been made including their use as maps, star charts, territorial markings or as some form of religious symbols. The nature of this type of art work is abstract and symbolic with there being no recognisable figures or images associated with the compositions. This presents a problem with understanding the purpose of these enigmatic symbols as their meaning is implied rather than stated as it would be with such as a written word. Also with being used over such a wide expanse of time, two thousand years, it is probable that the meaning of these markings will have changed as they became used in different contexts. The true meaning and purpose of this art can only be guessed at however it is generally considered that in some manner it is associated with the religious or belief systems of the Neolithic people.

The Carr Crags site itself is comprised of cup markings of various sizes and patterns and although there are no ring markings associated with them the sheer scale of the site is intriguing. The purpose of the site is obviously not known but in this specific instance is thought to have something to do with ritual practices. The location high on a hillside overlooking Teesdale and the altar reminiscent central stone may have influenced this conclusion but the size of the site and its composition would tend to preclude any more ordinary purpose such as a boundary marking. With the concentration of cup-markings at this small site this tends to imply that this location bore some great significance four thousand years ago.

Carr Crags is a site worth visiting for its own sake, it has an atmosphere of its own and in the right conditions can really set the mind thinking back to past times when the world was different.

A lollypop-shaped walk designed to give you as much time as possible to explore the carved stones at the ritual site. On the hillside it is very easy to spend over an hour locating and investigating all of the stones. Most of the walk is over open moor but surprisingly, considering Wainwright's opinion on the trees of Teesdale, this is the only walk in this book that includes a woodland section.

DISTANCE: 7.2 miles (11.5 km)
ASCENT: 1,493 feet (455 metres)
TERRAIN: Woodland and field path followed by open moorland. The

moorland section follows a rough quad bike track over open boggy ground with a section over pathless grassy tussocks.

TIME: 4 to 5 hours.

START: Bowlees Car Park (GR NY 908 283).

MAP: OL 31 North Pennines Teesdale & Weardale.

DOGS: Not allowed. For conservation reasons dogs are permanently excluded from this open access land.

ACCESS: The first half of the route is on public footpaths, the second half over open access land. There is normally a restriction on access mid-week from May to the early part of July due to ground nesting birds. Weekend access is normally still allowed. There is a stream crossing on this route that can be hazardous in times of bad weather when water levels are high.

Grid References

Bowlees car park	908 283
Stile in wall	907 290
Road crossing	910 302
Stream	912 319
Centre stone	919 320
James Hill	923 325
Bridge	913 319
Road crossing	910 302
Stile in wall	907 290
Bowlees car park	908 283

FGS Grading

Grading is F9 [D1, N2, T2, R2, H2]

Distance	1	6 – 12 miles
Navigation	2	Competent navigation skills needed
Terrain	2	25 -50% on graded track or path 50 – 75% off track
Remoteness	2	Countryside not in close proximity to habitation – less than 20% of the route within 2 miles
Height	2	Over 125 ft per mile

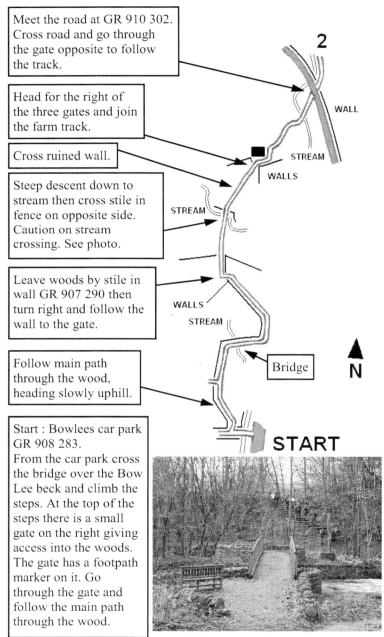

Meet the road at GR 910 302. Cross road and go through the gate opposite to follow the track.

Head for the right of the three gates and join the farm track.

Cross ruined wall.

Steep descent down to stream then cross stile in fence on opposite side. Caution on stream crossing. See photo.

Leave woods by stile in wall GR 907 290 then turn right and follow the wall to the gate.

Follow main path through the wood, heading slowly uphill.

Start : Bowlees car park GR 908 283.
From the car park cross the bridge over the Bow Lee beck and climb the steps. At the top of the steps there is a small gate on the right giving access into the woods. The gate has a footpath marker on it. Go through the gate and follow the main path through the wood.

2

WALL

STREAM

WALLS

STREAM

WALLS

STREAM

Bridge

N

START

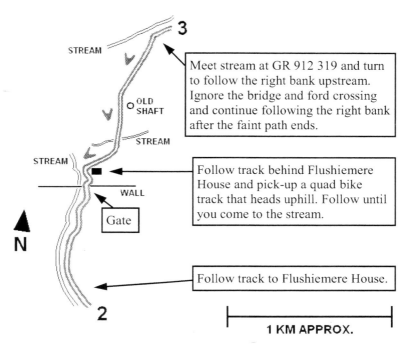

STREAM

3

Meet stream at GR 912 319 and turn to follow the right bank upstream. Ignore the bridge and ford crossing and continue following the right bank after the faint path ends.

OLD SHAFT

STREAM

STREAM

Follow track behind Flushiemere House and pick-up a quad bike track that heads uphill. Follow until you come to the stream.

WALL

Gate

N

Follow track to Flushiemere House.

2

|————————————————————|
1 KM APPROX.

The descent down to the stream crossing, also showing the route up to the farm of Broadley's Gate on the horizon.

Vehicle track cuts across the route just in front of the trig point. See the photo on page 12. After visiting the trig follow the track westwards and stay on it as it curves and starts to descend. In places the track is surfaced with wooden posts to provide a causeway on top of the peat.

James Hill summit. GR 923 325

From the Centre Stone head uphill on a compass bearing of 34°. There is no path and the going is rough. As you reach the summit plateau the watershed fence line comes into view which will help guide you to the trig point.

FENCE

4

N

Centre Stone GR 919 320. The marked stones form a keyhole shape around the centre stone.

STREAM 3

Follow the stream until your path is blocked by a deep gully. Follow the gully as it points you in the direction of the site of the stones.

First glimpse of the marked stones.

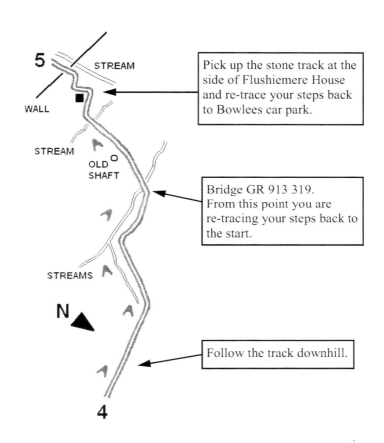

5 STREAM

WALL ■

STREAM

OLD ○
SHAFT

STREAMS

N▲

4

Pick up the stone track at the side of Flushiemere House and re-trace your steps back to Bowlees car park.

Bridge GR 913 319. From this point you are re-tracing your steps back to the start.

Follow the track downhill.

Looking back down the valley from the side of Flushiemere House.

WALK 4: MELDON HILL

Meldon Hill dominates the skyline above the Cow Green reservoir, the large whale-back looming large over the waters opposite the car park. Although still in Teesdale, technically this hill resides in Cumbria, the county border running down the middle of the reservoir at this point. Standing at 2,516 feet (767 metres) this is one of the larger hills that we encounter on these walks.

Unlike most of the hills in Teesdale the summit of Meldon is a nice grassy slope and not peat bog. However that is not to say that you wouldn't encounter the usual peat hags, its just that in this case they form a ring half-way up the hill and once you are past them the walking is a lot more comfortable.

This is a fairly longish walk, instead of heading straight up the front of Meldon, it takes the opportunity of following the Pennine Way deeper into Cumbria all the way to High Cup before turning round and approaching Meldon from the back. This is done purely and simply to see High Cup. For those of you who haven't seen this natural spectacle yet, you're missing one of the best sights in the North of England, a huge natural gouge in the Pennine range as if a handful of the hill has just been scooped away. The first sight of it as you come over High Cup Plain really takes the breath away and will stay with you for a very long time. It's a sight that I and now you will never tire of seeing. But take a tip and make sure that you go on a day with good visibility.

Turning back from High Cup the walk back climbs onto the summit of Meldon. This is a long walk through rough terrain with no path to guide you, real wilderness walking. There are a couple of false summits and it seems that the top of the hill is always moving away out of your reach but persevere and you will get there and be met by a cairn and the mangled remains of what was once a trig point. It's always a little bit sad when a trig literally falls apart, a bit like the demise of an old friend.

DISTANCE: 14.3 mile (22.8 km)
ASCENT: 1,765 feet (538 metres)
TERRAIN: The first and last mile and a half is on tarmac road leading down to the base of Cow Green dam. From there the Pennine Way is followed across the watershed to High Cup. The return leg up and over Meldon is across pathless open fell-side including peat hags and gullies.
TIME: 6 to 8 hours.
START: Cow Green reservoir car park. GR NY 811 309.

MAP: OL31 North Pennines Teesdale and Weardale.

OL19 Howgill Fells & Upper Eden Valley.

DOGS: Not allowed on the public access land which is part of the Moor House nature reserve.

ACCESS: The Pennine Way is on public rights of way but the route back up and over Meldon is on access land. Restrictions are placed during May to mid-July to limit access to weekends only for conservation reasons.

Grid References

Cow Green car park	811 309
Birkdale farm	804 278
Footbridge	766 268
High Cup	746 263
Pennine Way junction	743 262
Footbridge	749 270
Meldon Hill	771 291
Shooting huts	793 283
Birkdale farm	804 278
Cow Green car park	811 309

FGS Grading

Grading is F10 [D2, N2, T2, R3, H2]

Distance	2	12 – 18 miles
Navigation	2	Competent navigation skills needed
Terrain	2	25 -50% on graded track or path 50 – 75% off track
Remoteness	3	Remote, isolated location
Height	2	Over 125 ft per mile

Start : Cow Green reservoir car park. GR 811 309.

Leave the car park and walk back down the access road, see photo overleaf, until you come to the gravelled nature trail. Leave the road and turn right to follow this trail. At the end of the gravelled path turn left on to a track which heads to the tarmac access road which in turn leads to the dam. Turn right onto this road, go through the wooden gate and then follow the road to the bottom of the dam where you join the Pennine Way leading to Dufton.

2

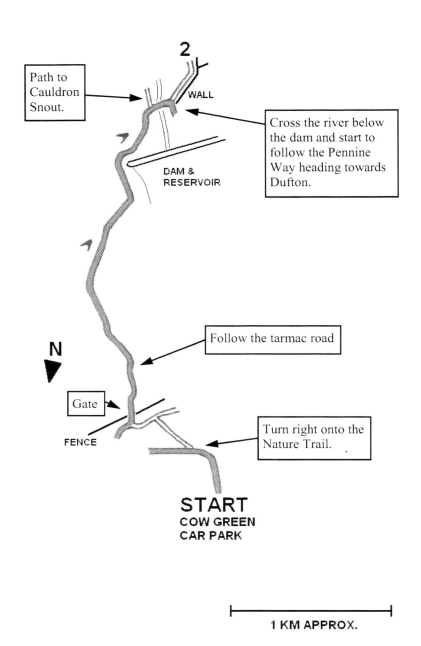

Path to Cauldron Snout.

WALL

Cross the river below the dam and start to follow the Pennine Way heading towards Dufton.

DAM & RESERVOIR

Follow the tarmac road

N

Gate

FENCE

Turn right onto the Nature Trail.

START
COW GREEN
CAR PARK

1 KM APPROX.

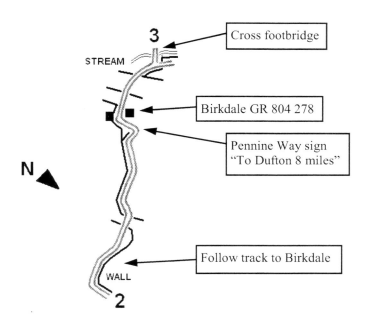

3

STREAM

Cross footbridge

Birkdale GR 804 278

Pennine Way sign
"To Dufton 8 miles"

N

Follow track to Birkdale

WALL

2

The start from the car park, looking back along the access road.

4

Bridge GR 766 268

OS map shows a bridleway leaving the Pennine Way to the left but the path does not exist on the ground.
Continue following the main Pennine Way.

MAIZE
BECK

Standing stones alongside the path mark the route of the Pennine Way.

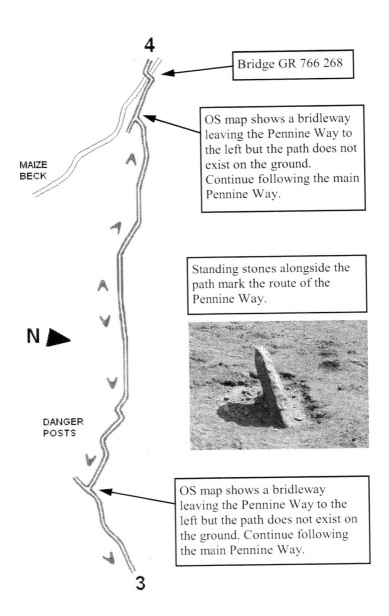

N ▶

DANGER
POSTS

OS map shows a bridleway leaving the Pennine Way to the left but the path does not exist on the ground. Continue following the main Pennine Way.

3

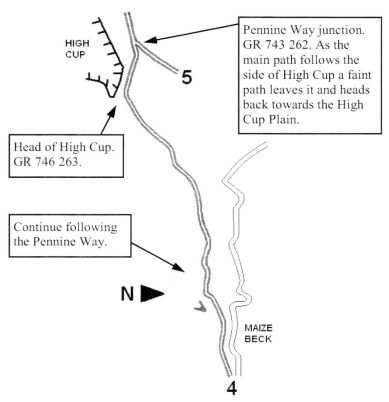

HIGH
CUP

5

Pennine Way junction.
GR 743 262. As the
main path follows the
side of High Cup a faint
path leaves it and heads
back towards the High
Cup Plain.

Head of High Cup.
GR 746 263.

Continue following
the Pennine Way.

N ▶

MAIZE
BECK

4

Showing the faint path heading towards Meldon from High Cup.

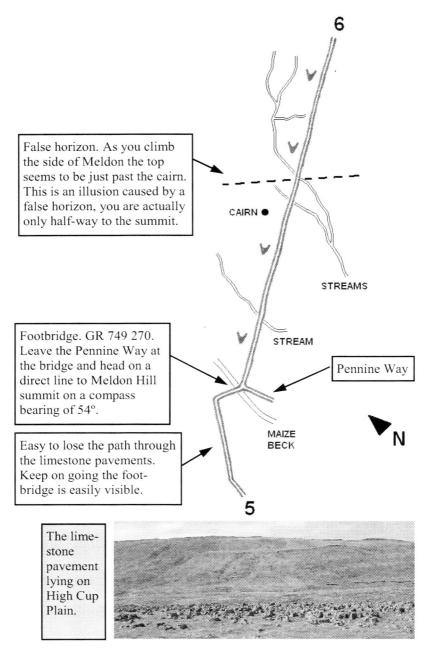

6

False horizon. As you climb
the side of Meldon the top
seems to be just past the cairn.
This is an illusion caused by a
false horizon, you are actually
only half-way to the summit.

CAIRN ●

STREAMS

STREAM

Pennine Way

Footbridge. GR 749 270.
Leave the Pennine Way at
the bridge and head on a
direct line to Meldon Hill
summit on a compass
bearing of 54°.

Easy to lose the path through
the limestone pavements.
Keep on going the foot-
bridge is easily visible.

MAIZE
BECK

N

5

The lime-
stone
pavement
lying on
High Cup
Plain.

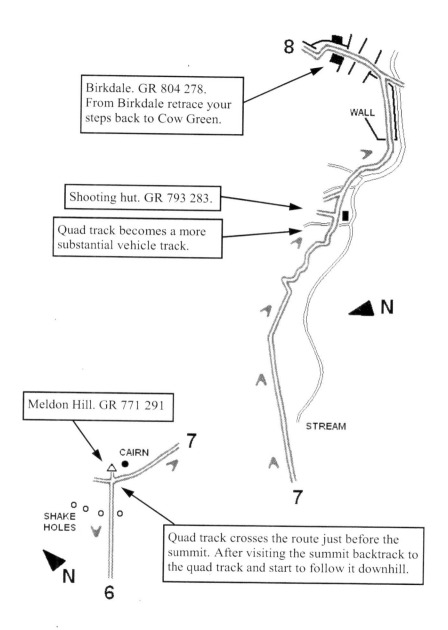

Birkdale. GR 804 278.
From Birkdale retrace your
steps back to Cow Green.

8

WALL

Shooting hut. GR 793 283.

Quad track becomes a more
substantial vehicle track.

N

Meldon Hill. GR 771 291

CAIRN
7

STREAM

7

o o o
SHAKE
HOLES

N

6

Quad track crosses the route just before the
summit. After visiting the summit backtrack to
the quad track and start to follow it downhill.

45

WALK 5: VIEWING HILL

The hardest summit to find of all the hills in this book. The summit in question is a wide plateau covered in bog and peat hags, which makes it very difficult to tell which part is the highest point. There is a small cairn but it is only small, about two foot high and this lies 100 metres to the south of the spot height of 569 metres shown on the Ordinance Survey map.

There is nothing spectacular at the top not even any really clear views, the broad expanse of the summit plateau stops them. This is one of those hills where there is not a lot of enjoyment in getting up but once you have, you can say that it has been done and tick it off your list.

Most walkers would tend to climb this hill from the Cow Green side which would be the easiest and most logical route. However easy and logic don't always mix with having a good day out on the hill. This route follows the length of the Harwood valley passing through the wonderfully named Howl of Harwood and Spitley Tongue before climbing the side of the hill and crossing the summit plateau.

DISTANCE: 7.6 mile (12.2 km)
ASCENT: 1,237 feet (377 metres)
TERRAIN: The first half of the route along the Harwood valley floor and up Spitley Tongue is all tarmac road and track. From the roadside of the B6277 the route crosses open fell-side complete with peat hags and gullies and is quite rough going.
TIME: 3 to 4 hours.
START: There is a small parking space next to the phone box where the road to Harwood descends from the B6277. If occupied there is a larger layby 100 metres further back towards Langdon Beck. GR NY 827 332.
MAP: OL31 North Pennines Teesdale and Weardale.
DOGS: There is a considerable stretch of road walking at the start and end of this walk. When coming back from the summit of the hill the route passes close to some disused shafts which, although fenced, an inquisitive dog might slip through so it is best to keep them under close control. There are sheep throughout the length of the route and cattle in some of the fields as you descend from the moor
ACCESS: The road, the Spitley Tongue track and the field paths coming back from the moor are all public rights of way. From the B6277 up and over the top of Viewing Hill is all over public access land.

Grid References

Parking space on B6277 road	827 332
B6277 road	794 350
Spot height	788 332
Summit cairn	789 332
Petergill Sike	801 330
Wall corner	808 332
Stile in wall	817 320
Footbridge	817 332
Road	817 336
Parking space	827 332

FGS Grading

Grading is F8 [D1, N2, T1, R2, H2]

Distance	1	6 – 12 miles
Navigation	2	Competent navigation skills needed
Terrain	1	50 – 75% on graded track or path 25 – 50% off track
Remoteness	2	Countryside not in close proximity to habitation – less than 20% of the route within 2 miles
Height	2	Over 125 ft per mile

Start : Car parking space alongside the B6277 road. GR 827 332.

From the car parking space head down the minor road going into the Harwood valley and follow the road along the valley floor. See photo below.

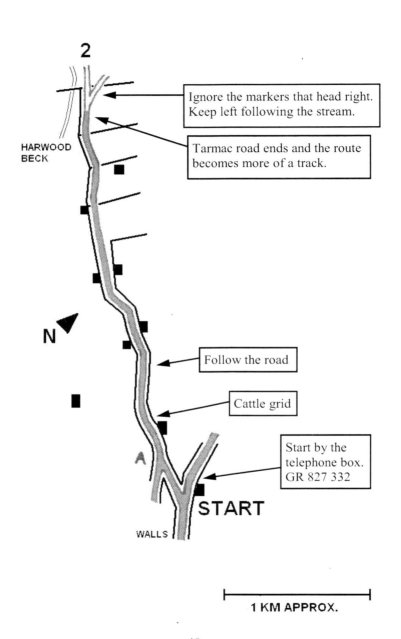

2

Ignore the markers that head right. Keep left following the stream.

Tarmac road ends and the route becomes more of a track.

HARWOOD BECK

N

Follow the road

Cattle grid

Start by the telephone box. GR 827 332

START

WALLS

1 KM APPROX.

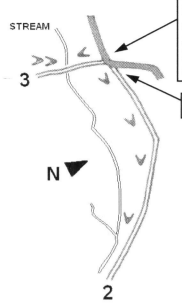

STREAM

3

N▼

2

From the first snow-pole on the side of the road take a bearing of 200° and head downhill to cross Harwood Beck and then up the other side.

Junction with road. GR 794 350

Looking across Harwood Beck and up the slopes of Viewing Hill from the roadside snow pole.

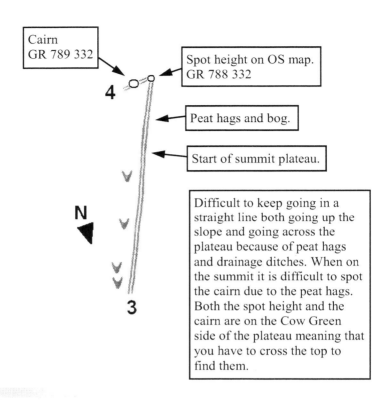

Cairn
GR 789 332

Spot height on OS map.
GR 788 332

4

Peat hags and bog.

Start of summit plateau.

N

Difficult to keep going in a
straight line both going up the
slope and going across the
plateau because of peat hags
and drainage ditches. When on
the summit it is difficult to spot
the cairn due to the peat hags.
Both the spot height and the
cairn are on the Cow Green
side of the plateau meaning that
you have to cross the top to
find them.

3

The small summit cairn on the top of Viewing Hill.

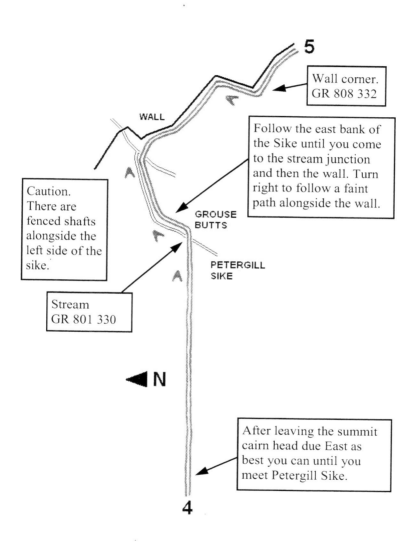

5

Wall corner.
GR 808 332

WALL

Follow the east bank of
the Sike until you come
to the stream junction
and then the wall. Turn
right to follow a faint
path alongside the wall.

Caution.
There are
fenced shafts
alongside the
left side of the
sike.

GROUSE
BUTTS

PETERGILL
SIKE

Stream
GR 801 330

◀ N

After leaving the summit
cairn head due East as
best you can until you
meet Petergill Sike.

4

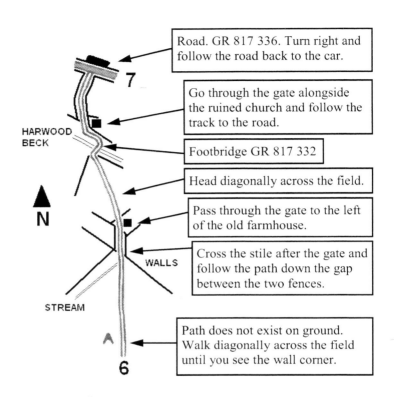

Road. GR 817 336. Turn right and follow the road back to the car.

Go through the gate alongside the ruined church and follow the track to the road.

Footbridge GR 817 332

Head diagonally across the field.

Pass through the gate to the left of the old farmhouse.

Cross the stile after the gate and follow the path down the gap between the two fences.

Path does not exist on ground. Walk diagonally across the field until you see the wall corner.

HARWOOD BECK

N

WALLS

STREAM

7

6

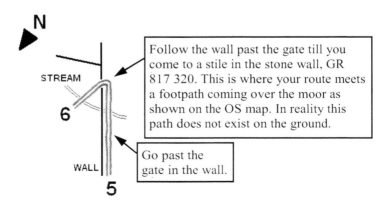

N

STREAM

WALL

6

5

Follow the wall past the gate till you come to a stile in the stone wall, GR 817 320. This is where your route meets a footpath coming over the moor as shown on the OS map. In reality this path does not exist on the ground.

Go past the gate in the wall.

WALK 6: THREE PIKES AND GREAT STONY HILL

A walk that crests two of the Teesdale hills, the only one in the book that does so. Both of these hills, Three Pikes and Great Stony Hill, are easily accessible from the main road that runs along the valley floor. However as with most of my walks I like to get value for money and a good day out in the hills and so this walk comes at them from a different side.

Three Pikes

An outlying hill set apart from the main Teesdale/Weardale watershed, it's summit lying definitely on the Teesdale side of the border fence. As with most of the Teesdale hills the summit is a large plateau area with a fair amount of bog and peat. The climb up the side of the hill from the road is the steepest of all the walks in this book, something that will really get the heart and legs pounding. Thankfully at this stage of the walk it is all on a relatively grassy slope, the bog and peat isn't encountered until you are actually on the summit itself.

There is no trig point on the top of Three Pikes although there is a small cairn positioned across the summit plateau overlooking down into the Tees valley. The cairn is on the "natural" approach to the summit coming straight up from the B6277 road on the Teesdale valley floor. With this walk approaching the summit from the other side of the hill it makes it necessary to cross the plateau to reach the cairn.

The cairn itself seems to be newly built, the stones are all clean and don't look aged as most cairns do. Alongside the cairn a couple of small walls

Old boundary stone alongside the fence leading upto Great Stony Hill.

53

have been built across the mouth of some depressions or shake holes, presumably to provide some form of rudimentary shelter in times of inclement weather but this may be a wrong conclusion. If you do know the answer, let me know - I'm curious.

Great Stony Hill

Alone among the Teesdale hills in having a small rocky outcrop surrounding it's summit. Don't get too overjoyed however as there is still plenty of peat on the way up but at least on the very top you get the opportunity to walk over some stone. You'll also notice the remains of walls and structures alongside the lofty trig point at the summit. Even at these exposed heights men have in the past, lived and worked and these walls and ruins mark a line of long disused mine workings.

This hill also has the distinction of being the only one along the Tees/ Wear watershed where you can look down from the top and see into both the valleys of Teesdale and Weardale without moving from the spot. On all the others the slope of the hill gets in the way and requires walking to one dale or the other to obtain a clear view.

On the OS map the summit of this hill is named as High Field and Great Stony Hill is shown further down on the Weardale side of the slope. However on the summit listings that make up the HEWITT peaks it is shown as Stony Hill and that is the name that has been used here.

DISTANCE: 8.9 mile (14.3 km)
ASCENT: 1,457 feet (444 metres)
TERRAIN: In the main open fell including peat hags and gullies. The second half of the route does involve some road and track walking.
TIME: 4 to 5 hours.
START: Road-side parking space alongside the Langden Beck to St John's Chapel road. GR NY 850 330.
MAP: OL31 North Pennines Teesdale and Weardale.
DOGS: If taking a dog on this walk be aware that the route does pass through some areas of old mines and shafts. There are also two stretches of road walking, one busier than the other in terms of traffic plus there are a number of stiles in the second half of the walk that may require your dog to be lifted over. You will encounter sheep throughout the length of the route and cattle in a couple of the fields passed through in the later stages.
ACCESS: The route uses access land right from the start of the walk. Public footpaths start to be used when the route crosses the B6277 and starts to

descend into the Harwood valley.

Grid References

Car park	850 330
Stream junction	848 338
Three Pikes cairn	834 343
Fence corner	834 348
Great Stony Hill/High Field	824 359
Road crossing	813 351
Junction with road	809 340
Lingy Hill	827 330
Road crossing	841 319
Junction with road	849 318
Car park	850 330

FGS Grading

Grading is F9 [D1, N2, T2, R2, H2]

Distance	1	6 – 12 miles
Navigation	2	Competent navigation skills needed
Terrain	2	25 -50% on graded track or path 50 – 75% off track
Remoteness	2	Countryside not in close proximity to habitation – less than 20% of the route within 2 miles
Height	2	Over 125 ft per mile

Start : Car parking area alongside the Langdon Beck-St John's Chapel road. GR 850 330.

From the car park, head behind the old railway wagons and follow the Langdon Beck upstream keeping to the left bank of the stream. See photo overleaf.

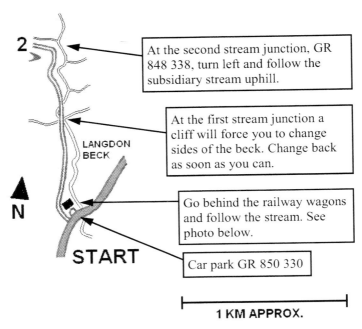

2

At the second stream junction, GR 848 338, turn left and follow the subsidiary stream uphill.

At the first stream junction a cliff will force you to change sides of the beck. Change back as soon as you can.

LANGDON BECK

N

Go behind the railway wagons and follow the stream. See photo below.

START

Car park GR 850 330

⊢——————————————⊣
1 KM APPROX.

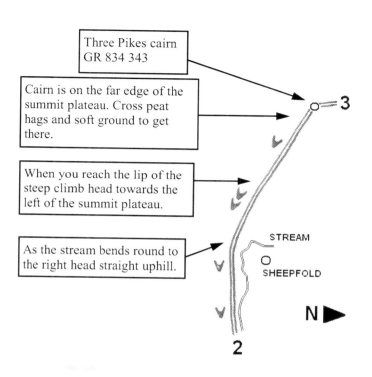

Three Pikes cairn
GR 834 343

Cairn is on the far edge of the
summit plateau. Cross peat
hags and soft ground to get
there.

3

When you reach the lip of the
steep climb head towards the
left of the summit plateau.

STREAM

As the stream bends round to
the right head straight uphill.

SHEEPFOLD

N ▶

2

Three Pikes summit with Great Stony Hill in the background.

Either retrace your steps back to Coldberry End and join the track there or alternatively head straight down but take care as you go through of the old mine workings.

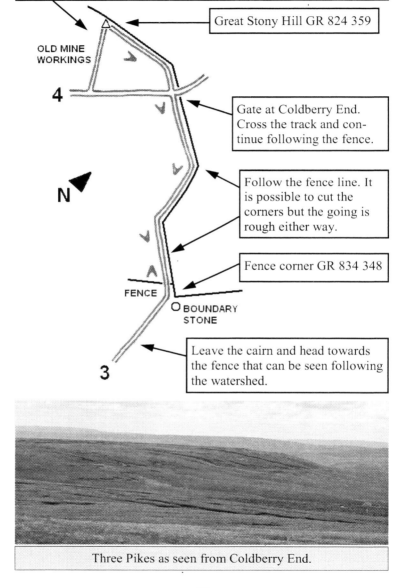

Great Stony Hill GR 824 359

OLD MINE WORKINGS

4

N

Gate at Coldberry End. Cross the track and continue following the fence.

Follow the fence line. It is possible to cut the corners but the going is rough either way.

Fence corner GR 834 348

FENCE

O BOUNDARY STONE

Leave the cairn and head towards the fence that can be seen following the watershed.

3

Three Pikes as seen from Coldberry End.

On the far side of the barn the route joins a waymarked walk. Turn left and follow the waymarkers alongside the stream.

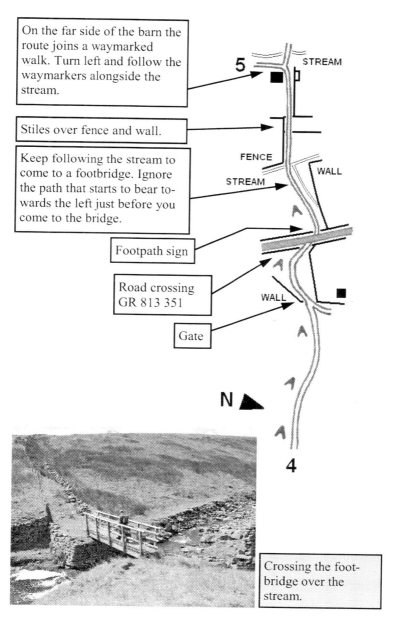

5 STREAM

Stiles over fence and wall.

FENCE

Keep following the stream to come to a footbridge. Ignore the path that starts to bear towards the left just before you come to the bridge.

STREAM

WALL

Footpath sign

Road crossing GR 813 351

WALL

Gate

N ▲

4

Crossing the footbridge over the stream.

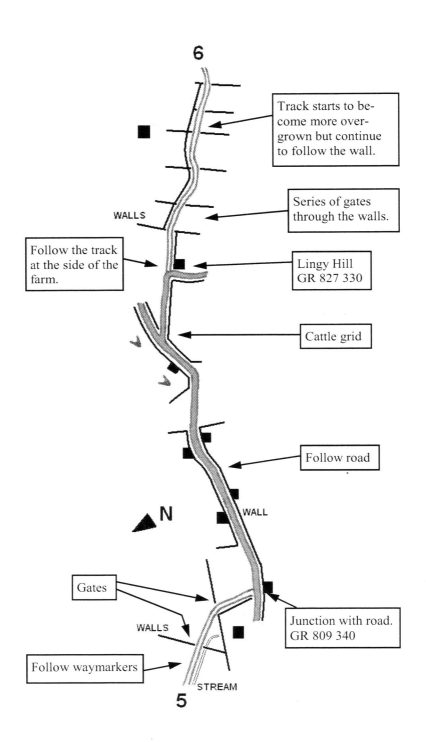

6

Track starts to become more overgrown but continue to follow the wall.

WALLS

Series of gates through the walls.

Follow the track at the side of the farm.

Lingy Hill
GR 827 330

Cattle grid

Follow road

▲N

WALL

Gates

WALLS

Junction with road.
GR 809 340

Follow waymarkers

STREAM

5

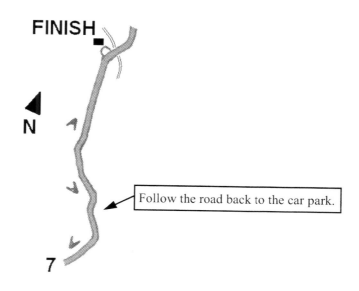

FINISH

N

Follow the road back to the car park.

7

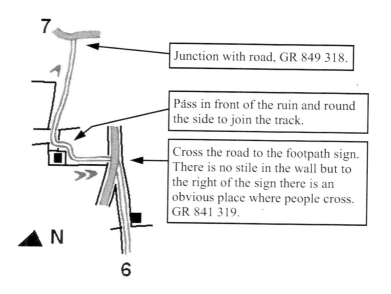

7

Junction with road, GR 849 318.

Páss in front of the ruin and round the side to join the track.

Cross the road to the footpath sign. There is no stile in the wall but to the right of the sign there is an obvious place where people cross. GR 841 319.

N

6

WALK 7: BURNHOPE SEAT

Burnhope Seat, a small grassy knoll surrounded by a long, uphill peaty morass. I'd forgotten what a total pain it is getting to the top until I came to field-test this book. But when you get to the top - what a view. Totally worth it. On one side across the Tees valley the high hills of the Pennines, Little Dun Fell, Dun Fell and the whale-back that is Cross Fell. On the other, looking down into Weardale across Burnhope Reservoir, a smaller cousin of Cow Green.

For centuries this was the highest point in the old traditional County Durham then when the local government reorganisations of the 1970's changed the county boundaries land south of the Tees that was part of Yorkshire became part of Durham and this included Mickle Fell. As a result Burnhope lost it's claim as top hill to the new interloper.

This route is an out and back walk but don't decry it for that, as with most walks in this part of the county there is a completely different perspective when walking the outward leg compared to coming back towards home. At times it is difficult to believe that you have actually al-

The infant River Tees on its way down from the slopes of Cross Fell.

ready walked the same route just a few hours before.

The majority of the route is along an old miner's track that makes it's way beyond Cow Green with views of the infant river Tees as it flows down from its birthplace on the slopes of Cross Fell before it is held back in the giant reservoir . This is as far up Teesdale as you can get without some serious off-path walking, but there again that is a different walk for another day.

The miner's track may be a well-surfaced man-made track but it penetrates deep into the wilderness of Upper Teesdale. Here you can appreciate the landscape that has been made here in these high hills and how special it is. The land in front is all part of Moor House Nature Reserve, a site of international importance.

DISTANCE: 11.5 mile (18.4 km)
ASCENT: 971 feet (296 metres)
TERRAIN: Old miner's track leading to a road crossing. From the crossing the route covers open fell-side complete with peat hags and gullies. Very rough going.
TIME: 5 to 6 hours.
START: Cow Green reservoir car park. GR NY 811 309.
MAP: OL31 North Pennines Teesdale and Weardale.
DOGS: As far as I'm aware there are no restrictions although don't expect them to come back clean. There is one stile which is crossed twice where they will need to be lifted over and the road crossing can be busy during the height of summer. Obviously there are sheep throughout the full length of the route.
ACCESS: The old miner's track is a public footpath all the way upto the road crossing. From the crossing the route travels over public access land.

Grid References

Cow Green car park	811 309
Track/road junction	784 353
Scraith Head	791 369
Burnhope Seat	788 375
Scraith Head	791 369
Track/road junction	784 353
Cow Green car park	811 309

FGS Grading

Grading is F6 [D1, N2, T1, R2, H0]

Distance	1	6 – 12 miles
Navigation	2	Competent navigation skills needed
Terrain	1	50 – 75% on graded track or path 25 – 50% off track
Remoteness	2	Countryside not in close proximity to habitation – less than 20% of the route within 2 miles
Height	0	Less than 100 ft per mile

Start : Cow Green reservoir car park. GR 811 309.

Head out of the bottom end of the car park, round the gate and onto the old miner's track. Follow the obvious main track for the next four miles until you come to the B6277 road. See photo below.

2

1 KM APPROX.

Follow the main track. See photo above.

N

Cow Green car park GR 811 309

START

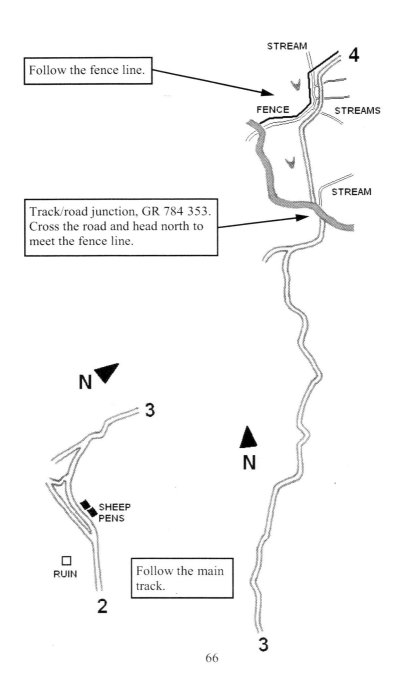

Follow the fence line.

STREAM

4

FENCE

STREAMS

STREAM

Track/road junction, GR 784 353.
Cross the road and head north to
meet the fence line.

N▼

3

▲
N

SHEEP
PENS

☐
RUIN

Follow the main
track.

2

3

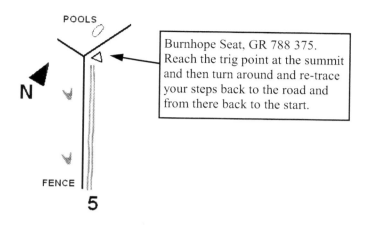

POOLS

Burnhope Seat, GR 788 375.
Reach the trig point at the summit
and then turn around and re-trace
your steps back to the road and
from there back to the start.

N

FENCE

5

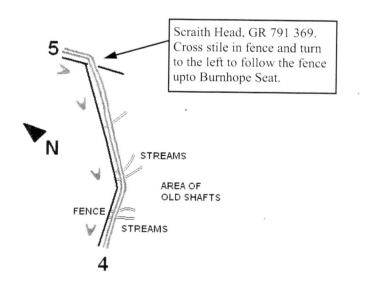

Scraith Head, GR 791 369.
Cross stile in fence and turn
to the left to follow the fence
upto Burnhope Seat.

5

N

STREAMS

AREA OF
OLD SHAFTS

FENCE

STREAMS

4

WALK 8: MICKLE FELL

Mickle Fell, the forbidden summit that is hidden behind danger signs but which also happens to be the highest point in County Durham.

Despite the fact that it is set right in the middle of the vast tract of Ministry of Defence land that makes up Warcop ranges, it is possible to visit the summit of this high hill. With permission of the MOD access is allowed on certain days throughout the year although there is a pre-defined route that you must follow and there are other restrictions and limitations that apply. For more details on obtaining permission to visit the summit see the section on Access and the Right to Roam towards the front of this book.

The route of this walk is pretty straight-forward, the MOD don't want you to wander aimlessly over their land and so the path stays close to an easily followed fence-line. However the path is not exactly well-trodden, the warning signs both on the ground and on the map tend to put off most walkers. But don't be fooled by dreams of isolation, of all the hills in Teesdale this is the one where you are most likely to meet other walkers, albeit only small numbers, purely because as there are only a limited number of days that you can go up the hill then everybody is restricted to these same few days.

The summit of Mickle is different to all the others gained in this book having a short, close-cropped grassy surface with hardly a glimpse of peat in sight although you still see plenty of that while climbing up to the summit plateau. It also has one of the biggest stone cairns that I've seen on any summit. As you walk towards it across the plateau it looks like one huge rock sticking out of the ground but as you get closer you can slowly start to see that it is actually made up of smaller individual stones piled together to rise close to eight foot above the surface.

As you'll gather from looking at the OS map, this walk does involve leaving the Pennine Way to cross Maize Beck in order to reach the bottom of Mickle Fell and start the climb proper. Be aware that there is no bridge or other easy crossing of the beck. Crossing over the stream involves negotiating your way over a jumble of stones sticking out of the water. There is a strong likelihood of getting your feet wet. In times of bad weather when water levels are running high this crossing does have the potential to be dangerous so never underestimate it. It was the deaths of two walkers in a flooded Maize Beck that was the catalyst for the formation of the local mountain rescue team, Teesdale and Weardale Search and Mountain Rescue, in the late 1960's.

DISTANCE: 11.5 mile (18.4 km)
ASCENT: 1,647 feet (502 metres)
TERRAIN: The first and last mile and a half is on tarmac road leading down to the base of the Cow Green dam. The Pennine Way is then followed for just over a mile before striking-off over open fell to reach the summit of Mickle Fell. This route does involve the crossing of Maize Beck which during and shortly after bad weather does have the potential to be hazardous.
TIME: 4.5 to 6 hours.
START: Cow Green reservoir car park. GR NY 811 309.
MAP: OL31 North Pennines Teesdale and Weardale.
     OL19 Howgill Fells & Upper Eden Valley.
DOGS: Not allowed on the MOD land.
ACCESS: By prior arrangement with the MOD. See the Access section towards the front of the book for further details.

Grid References

Cow Green car park	811 309
Birkdale farm	804 278
Old mine workings/flagpost	796 273
Cairn	795 267
Stream crossing	791 263
Fence and gate	801 242
Mickle Fell summit	806 245

Return using the same grid references in reverse.

FGS Grading

Grading is F9 [D1, N2, T2, R2, H2]

Distance	1	6 – 12 miles
Navigation	2	Competent navigation skills needed
Terrain	2	25 -50% on graded track or path 50 – 75% off track
Remoteness	2	Countryside not in close proximity to habitation – less than 20% of the route within 2 miles
Height	2	Over 125 ft per mile

As with a number of the hills in this country Mickle Fell has had its incidents with low-flying aircraft. On the night of 18th October 1944 a Stirling bomber flew into the top of Mickle Fell. The crew were on their final navigation training flight before being posted to operational duties in the air war over Germany. Flying from their base in Cambridgeshire the aircraft strayed off the planned route in thick fog and at roughly 01:00 hours hit the top of the Fell. On impact one of the plane's wings was torn off and the plane cart-wheeled over the ridge line and crashed upside down on the south side of the hill.

Sadly out of a crew of seven, six New Zealanders and one Englishman, only one survived. Unlike the other crew members who were located towards the front of the plane and received the full force of the impact, the tail gunner was thrown clear when the plane hit. Although injured he somehow made his way in the dark and over rough country to summon help at the nearest farm some two miles away. It is not known which farm this was but was probably Birkdale which you pass through on the walk.

Start : Cow Green reservoir car park. GR 811 309.
Leave the car park and walk back down the access road, see photo below, until you come to the gravelled nature trail. Leave the road and turn right to follow this trail. At the end of the gravelled path turn left on to a track which heads to the tarmac access road which in turn leads to the dam. Turn right onto this road, go through the wooden gate and then follow the road to the bottom of the dam where you join the Pennine Way leading to Dufton.

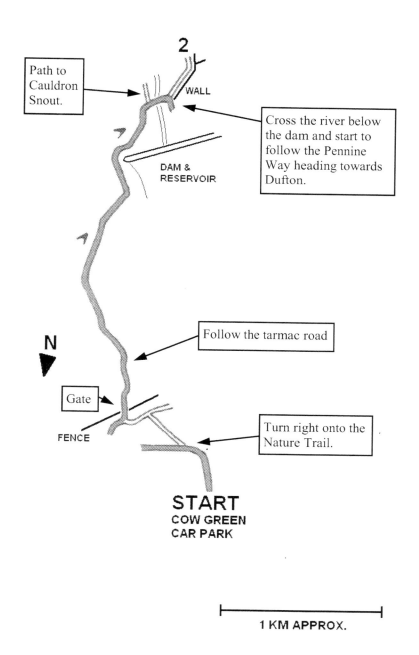

2

Path to Cauldron Snout.

WALL

Cross the river below the dam and start to follow the Pennine Way heading towards Dufton.

DAM & RESERVOIR

N

Follow the tarmac road

Gate

FENCE

Turn right onto the Nature Trail.

START
COW GREEN
CAR PARK

1 KM APPROX.

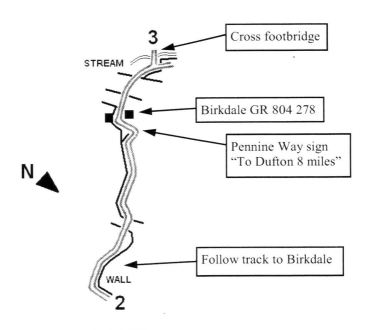

3 Cross footbridge

STREAM

Birkdale GR 804 278

Pennine Way sign
"To Dufton 8 miles"

N▲

Follow track to Birkdale

WALL
2

Mickle Fell looming behind Birkdale Farm.

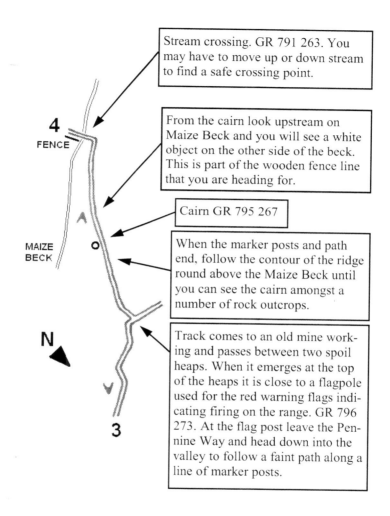

Stream crossing. GR 791 263. You may have to move up or down stream to find a safe crossing point.

From the cairn look upstream on Maize Beck and you will see a white object on the other side of the beck. This is part of the wooden fence line that you are heading for.

Cairn GR 795 267

When the marker posts and path end, follow the contour of the ridge round above the Maize Beck until you can see the cairn amongst a number of rock outcrops.

Track comes to an old mine working and passes between two spoil heaps. When it emerges at the top of the heaps it is close to a flagpole used for the red warning flags indicating firing on the range. GR 796 273. At the flag post leave the Pennine Way and head down into the valley to follow a faint path along a line of marker posts.

4
FENCE

MAIZE
BECK

N

3

Once the summit has been visited return back to Cow Green by the same route.

Follow summit ridge for 600 metres to arrive at the large summit cairn.

King's Pot. Edge of a deep escarpment overlooking King's Pot. See photo on page 82.

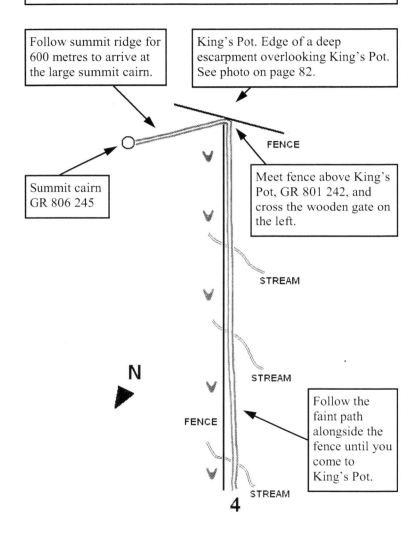

FENCE

Summit cairn
GR 806 245

Meet fence above King's Pot, GR 801 242, and cross the wooden gate on the left.

STREAM

STREAM

N

FENCE

Follow the faint path alongside the fence until you come to King's Pot.

STREAM

4

Moor House Nature Reserve.

The landscape of Upper Teesdale is one that is not just unique in Britain but internationally as well. This was recognised in 1952 when the Moor House area was part of the first group of national nature reserves created in this country. Since then the 3,497 hectares that comprise England's highest and largest reserve have also become a United Nations Biosphere Reserve and a European Special Protection Area reflecting the world importance of this region.

Within this protected environment lie a varied number of different environments including blanket bog, upland grasslands, pastures, hay meadows and deciduous woodland. Each of these areas has its own distinct flora and fauna including the renowned "Teesdale assemblage" of artic-alpine plants many of which can only be found elsewhere in this country in the sub-tundra conditions of the Cairngorm plateau.

The reserve covers a wide area stretching from the slopes of Cross Fell where the source of the Tees rises all the way downstream to the High Force waterfall. In the west it extends over the summits of Great Dun Fell, Little Dun Fell and Knock Fell and down to the upper edges of the enclosed land in the Eden Valley in Cumbria. Several of the walks in this book are either totally in or partially cross the reserve.

The expanse of Moor House lying beneath the slopes of Dun Fell and Cross Fell.

APPENDIX

Using the Route Diagrams

The author of this book uses strip diagrams to illustrate the route to be followed with attached notes to provide further detail.

The diagrams are based on strips, meaning that you follow one strip from start to finish and then start the next strip. From the "Start" follow the route up to the number "2" position at the top of the strip. The number "2" position then becomes the bottom start of the next strip. This strip is then followed up to the number "3" position at the top which in turn becomes the bottom start of the next strip, etc, etc.

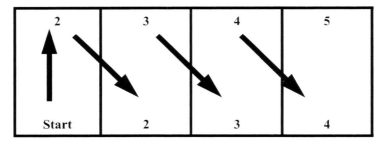

Unlike Ordnance Survey maps, symbols have been kept to a minimum in order to keep the diagrams as simple as possible. The main ones used are arrows to indicate whether you are travelling uphill or downhill. The use of two arrows indicates a steeper gradient. The point of the arrow will always indicate the bottom of the slope. Also used are black squares to indicate the location of buildings.

Ferguson Grading System (`FGS`)

1. Introduction
The FGS has been adopted as a means of assessing the nature and severity of the various walks in this book and the abilities and equipment needed to tackle each one safely. The FGS was developed by Stuart Ferguson, a long time fell and trail runner, climber, mountaineer, mountainbiker and general outdoor enthusiast. In the opinion of Trailguides the FGS is the most accurate and comprehensive grading system for compar-

ing off-road walking, running and mountain-biking routes anywhere in the country.

2. The System

Tables 1 & 2, set out below, are used in order to give a grading to each route. Table 1 sets out three categories of country that a route could potentially cross, together with a range of factors that would need to be considered when tackling that route. The three categories are, Trail, Fell and Mountain, and after assessing which category best fits the route, a letter, either `T`, `F` or `M`, is allocated to that route. Where a route does not fit perfectly into one of the three categories the closest category is allocated.

Table 2 deals with five specific aspects of the route namely distance, navigation, terrain, remoteness and height gain, and each one is allocated a letter, `D`, `N`, `T`, `R`, and `H`. Each letter is also given a severity score from the range 0-3 or 0-4, in respect of distance (`D`). The higher the number, the more severe the route. The five severity scores are then added together to give an overall score. The overall score is then put with the Table 1 category letter (i.e. `T`, `F` or `M`).

In order to show how the grading has been determined for each walk in this book, the five individual severity scores are set out, in square brackets, immediately after the actual grading. So, for example, Walk 6 Three Pikes and Great Stony Hill has a grading of F9 [D1, N2, T2, R2, H2], indicating that it is a Fell Category walk with a total severity score of 9. This is made up of the five specific severity scores, for distance (`D`), navigation (`N`), terrain (`T`), remoteness (`R`) and height gain (`H`), of 1, 2, 2, 2 and 2 respectively. The highest total severity score which can be achieved is 16 and the lowest total severity score achievable is 0.

The table which accompanies the grading at the start of each walk sets out the specific factors, extracted from Table 2, that need to be considered when tackling that particular walk.

TABLE 1

	TRAIL	FELL	MOUNTAIN
Description	Lowland and forest areas including urban, cultivated and forested locations.	Moorlands and upland areas which may include some upland cultivated and forestry areas plus possibly remote locations.	Upland and mountain areas including remote and isolated locations.
Height	Not usually above 1,000 feet but may go up to 2,500 feet	Usually above 1,000 feet, up to 2,500 feet and above.	Usually above 2,500 feet and up to 4,000 feet.
Way-marking	Usually	Limited	None
Terrain	Usually graded paths, tracks and trails but may include some off-trail	May include some graded paths, tracks and trails but mainly off-trail	Virtually all off-trail
Height gain	Limited height gain	May include considerable height gain	May include some severe height gain.
Effects of weather	Very limited effect	May be prone to sudden weather changes	Extreme weather a possibility
Navigational skills	None to basic	Basic to competent	Competent to expert
Equipment	Walking shoes/boots. Possibly waterproofs Food and drink dependant upon route.	3/4 season walking boots. Full waterproof cover. Possibly map and compass dependant upon route. Food and drink dependant upon route.	Mountain boots. Full waterproof cover. Map and compass. Food and drink
Escape Routes	Yes	Some	Some to nil

TABLE 2

Score	0	1	2	3	4
Distance	Up to 6 miles	6 – 12 miles	12 – 18 miles	18 miles +	24 miles +
Navigation	No navigation skills needed	Basic navigation skills needed	Competent navigation skills needed	Expert navigation skills needed	
Terrain	75% + on graded track or path	50 – 75% on graded track or path 25 – 50% off track	25 -50% on graded track or path 50 – 75% off track	Under 25% on graded track or path Over 75% off track	
Remoteness	Urban	Countryside in fairly close proximity to habitation – at least 80% of the route within 2 miles	Countryside not in close proximity to habitation – less than 20% of the route within 2 miles	Remote, isolated location	
Height gain	Less than 100 ft per mile	Over 100 ft per mile	Over 125 ft per mile	Over 250 ft per mile	

Notes to Table 1

Graded paths = Well established paths with a stable surface.

Escape routes = The opportunity to cut the route short and return to the start without completing the full course in the event of weather changes or unforeseen incidents.

The Author

Keven Shevels

Kev has been involved with outdoor sports since his school days doing the Duke of Edinburgh award, spending his time either walking or running and latterly mountain biking through the countryside of the North East and beyond. He is not ashamed to admit that he is one of these boring people who can sit and spend hours reading a map the way that other people read a book. His great delight is coming up with new routes that he can subsequently explore and investigate.

Like many walkers he has always had a fascination with the high places and while not having a compulsive tick-off mentality he often seeks out the summits just to see what is there and what the view from the top is like. This in-built curiosity to go and view things that spark his interest and his knowledge of the Durham Dales landscape makes him a perfect guide to take you around the summits of the High Hills of Teesdale.

Now in his fifties Kev has been unable to continue his running due to injury problems but instead has been co-author of one of the most innovative series of coaching books for fell and trail runners in recent years. He now brings his easy to read, informative style of writing to guide books for those who walk in the countryside of County Durham, his home county.

The author descending on the wooden track-way. Walk 3. James Hill.

Trailguides Limited

Trailguides Limited is a small independent publisher specialising in books and other publications for outdoor people. Being based in Darlington we pride ourselves in producing unique guide books for those who walk in our home county of Durham. Our aim is to produce guides that are as user-friendly, easy to use and provide as much information as possible and all in an entertaining manner. In short to increase the enjoyment of the user and to showcase the very best of the great North Eastern countryside and to highlight, in particular, the special features on any trail that otherwise might so easily be missed.

The Durham Walker Series of books explores the heritage of us all and lets you see your county with new eyes. These books are written to not just take you on a walk but to investigate, explore and understand the objects, places and history that you will encounter on the route.

If you've enjoyed following the routes in this guide and want news and details of other routes that are being developed by Trailguides then look at the company website at
www.trailguides.co.uk

Comments and, yes, criticisms, are always welcomed especially if you discover a change to a route. Contact us by email through the website or by post at Trailguides Limited, 35 Carmel Road South, Darlington, Co Durham DL3 8DQ.

Part of the caves at High Hurth Edge. Walk 2. Fendrith Hill.

The escarpment above King's Pot. Walk 8. Mickle Fell.

Acknowledgements.

Thanks are due to Harry Manuel, more often than not my walking companion on these "little" excursions into the wilds of Teesdale. He also ended up being the main model on a number of the photos.

Disclaimer

The information contained in these pages and the route descriptions is provided in good faith, but no warranty is made for its accuracy. The contents are, at the time of writing and to the best of our knowledge, up-to-date and correct. However, the world is a changing environment and what is correct one day may not be so the next. Care should always be taken when following these route descriptions just as it should when following maps or way-markers of any kind.

No guarantee whatsoever is provided by the author and/or Trailguides Limited and no liability is accepted for any loss, damage or injury of any kind resulting from the use of this book, nor as a result of any defect or inaccuracy in it.

As with all outdoor activities, you and you alone are responsible for your safety and well being.

A. Glen Shoggle

OS Map ref. start: 352919
Terrain: Easy, some moderately steep sections
Access: Take the A3 (TT Course) to Ballaugh, turn right by the Raven pub and follow the minor road for a mile. There is a parking area by the entrance to Ballaugh plantation. Ballaugh is on a frequent bus route.

A forest walk following a stream along a valley with commanding views across the Irish Sea. There are lower level routes for easier walking. (The different routes are shown on 1:25,000 map).

Enter Ballaugh Plantation by the gate, there is an information board displaying a variety of paths that can be walked, as well as the mountain bike route. Ballaugh is a large plantation of Sitka spruce and Japanese larch planted in 1959-67. It is actively managed and there are areas where trees have been felled to provide timber. Continue forwards on the main track to an information board about Glen Shoggle by a wood carving of a raven.

Bear left and ford the stream (if the water is too deep take the path on the right which leads to a bridge that crosses over the stream). Bear right along a wide path with the stream on the right, this lower section is marked with a 'River Ramble' sign. Continue on passing a

Carving of a raven

pond which has an information board nearby. Follow path round the pond and up a flight of steps where there is a bridge to a second pond.

The path heads through the trees passing a water cascade. By a bench is a bare tree trunk which has a bend in it where the tree looks as if it grew downwards before resuming normal upwards growth. When the path joins a main track bear right and head further up the valley passing another small water cascade. The path crosses a clearing and becomes a little steeper, continue forwards across a track: the stream is now a distance below.

The path briefly emerges from the trees and passes a track on the left. The path bends right, continue uphill passing a turning, there are now open views west across the Irish Sea. Pass another turning and return into the forest, the path levels off and slopes downhill. Cross over another path ('Ginger's Run'), at the bottom turn right, now the path slopes downhill quite steeply. At a fork bear right heading more towards the trees and the stream.

Continue forwards, at the time of writing a beetle survey was in progress. At a crossing of paths bear left to temporarily re-join the earlier route. Bear left over the stream then right passing the two ponds. Continue forwards to the plantation entrance gates.

The Glen Dhoo walk can be accessed from the same car park.

B. Glen Dhoo

OS Map ref. start: 352919
Terrain: Easy
Access: Take the A3 (TT Course) to Ballaugh, turn right by the Raven pub and follow the minor road for a mile. There is a parking area by the entrance to Ballaugh plantation. Ballaugh is on a frequent bus route.

A walk through remote countryside along a tranquil valley, several tholtans (derelict farm buildings) are evidence that it was once a thriving farming community.

Glen Dhoo. Glen Dhoo translates from Manx as the 'Dark Glen' - so called because of the shadow cast by Sileau Curn. The area is owned by the Manx Wildlife Trust who actively manage the lower slopes to encourage plant diversity while leaving the upper slopes alone. A farm settlement used to exist up until the late 19th century. High up on the hills are hut circles associated with high pasture of animals in the summer. The remains of an old mill and dam, together with a tholtan known as The Phurt are next to the stream. In the 1841 Census this is recorded as a thriving community comprising farmers, a weaver, a nailer, a wool spinner and a tailor – although it is likely that the men supplemented their income by fishing in the summer. The last person to have lived here left in the early 1920s.

From the car park walk back down the road to a Greenway track sign 'Bayr Glas' on the left. The track climbs gently and in a couple of hundred yards the wooded slopes of the hills that surround the valley start to be seen. There are bright yellow coconut-scented gorse, primroses and bluebells in the spring. The path rises and falls but never steeply so.

On the right there is a 4 foot high vertical slate with hole which was probably the gatepost of the farm that lies further along. The path can become a little muddy for a few yards as a small brook crosses over to the main stream. Proceed through two gates, the second of which marks the entrance to the Manx Nature Conservation Trust Reserve.

Cross the stream by the stepping stones, or the large slate slab, over to the tholtan where there is an information board. It is a two-storey building dating back to the 18th century with a hearth at either end: it is quite a grand building for such a remote location. The area around the house used to have 10 buildings. Continue along the grassy path past more examples of derelict farm buildings and walls (many now grassed over). On the left there is a rusted wheel which indicates that there was a small water mill here: traces of the mill race (channel) and mill pond can be seen. Climb over the stile to pass further old structures – the building on the right, with a massive tree trunk leaning against it, is quite substantial.

This is a good place pause and absorb how isolated it must have been living here before turning around and retracing one's steps.

The Glen Shoggle walk can be accessed from the same car park.

Tholtan in Glen Dhoo

C. Cornaa Glen

OS Map ref. start: 467897
Terrain: Easy
Access: A few miles south of Ramsey on the coast road (A2) turn left onto A15 at the Hibernian, after a mile take the first right which leads across Manx Electric Railway (MER) tracks to a car park on the right by the entrance to Ballaglass Glen. There is a MER stop at Cornaa .

A wooded walk along the Raad ny Foillan down Cornaa valley to the beach at Port Cornaa

Leave the car park and turn right down the road, just before the bridge turn left at footpath sign for Port Cornaa. After a brief climb turn right onto a downhill track – this is the Raad ny Foillan. At a gap in the trees on the right one can see across the valley and up to North Barrule. Keep on the track passing driveways to private houses. Cross over a stile, the track is now in a more densely wooded area.

At a fork in the path detour briefly to the right to open ground by the river – a popular picnic spot. Return back to the main path which passes derelict buildings.

Carl Lamm's Explosives Factory. In 1885 a Swedish chemist, Carl Lamm, invented Bellite, a new form of explosive which was impossible to detonate without a specific detonator. This made it much safer than dynamite that could easily explode by impact, misuse or extreme heat. Lamm wanted to manufacture his new product in the UK but there were very strict

View towards North Barrule

regulations in place regarding its manufacture. No such rules on the production of explosives currently applied on Isle of Man, so he commenced the construction of this factory. However, the Manx Government began to have concerns about safety. They sought advice from the UK, who recommended that the same safety regulations should be applied as in UK. These would make the production process uneconomic, so he never completed the factory.

Cross the river by the bridge and head towards a smaller bridge on the right to pick up the path to Port Cornaa beach. The beach is formed of storm-tossed pebbles and rocks and so is constantly shifting its shape. It is gradually growing in height as the storm tides lift stones off the bottom and hurl them up the beach.

Return to Ballaglass Glen by the same route, remembering to turn left when a small gully crosses the path by a footpath sign.

Cornaa River

D. Glen Mooar (by Glen Maye)

OS Map ref. start: 235798
Terrain: Easy
Access: Glen Mooar is on A27 about 5 miles south of Peel, there is a car park by the Glen Maye National Glen and Waterfall Inn (closed). There is an occasional bus service.

The walk follows the Bayr ny Skeddan for a couple of miles along a scenic valley, initially through woodland then across open countryside with hill views.

Leave the car park and turn right downhill, at the bottom there is a very small footpath sign pointing left down a narrow access – if you have reached Sound Road turn back as you have gone too far. In parts this section of the path looks like one is walking through someone's garden. The path widens into a larger track, follow the blue Bayr ny Skeddan way-marker which takes one off to the left through trees.

Bayr ny Skeddan. This translates from Manx as 'The Herring Road'. It is a 14 mile long footpath from Castletown Harbour to Peel which follows an ancient packhorse route taken by fishermen between two key ports. Legend has it that some used the distraction of the smell of herring to take smuggled spirits away from the port where they came in.

The path crosses a river by a concrete bridge and follows by the river through woodland. At a junction with another track turn right, passing a picnic area on the right. The track ascends and passes an entrance to Arrasey Forest, well-used by mountain bikers. Continue straight along the track, the river is now a considerable distance below on the right. At a fork bear right onto the lower, unmade track with views of South Barrule directly in front. The track descends to the same level as the river, with small streams feeding in from the left making the path wet and muddy.

At a fork in the path indicated by a bridleway sign the Glen Mooar path has come to an end - one can turn round to return to the start. (The right fork is the continuation of the Bayr ny Skeddan which leads away from the river into Glen Rushen: this path ends at a road in about 1½ miles).

Looking north to Glen Mooar

E. Port Jack Glen

OS Map ref. start: 399773
Terrain: Easy
Access: Follow Douglas Prom north, as you climb the hill turn left immediately after Port Jack Chippy, turn left again and park nearby. The lower entrance to the glen is just behind the row of shops on the corner. There is a bus stop near the shops.

A peaceful and attractive park in a residential area with paved walks by a stream.

Until Onchan Commissioners took control in 1959 the area was simply an undeveloped and overgrown valley at the foot of Royal Avenue. Subsequently it has been landscaped with paths, bridges and steps with plantings of bushes and flowering plants. The stream has been dug out to form to small ponds. There is a circular path to the top of the glen, where this is a shelter, and a path back down.

Onchan Internment Camp. The houses on both sides of the glen formed Onchan Internment Camp, housing nearly 1,300 German and Austrian alien civilians during World War II. The surrounding streets were fenced with barbed wire. The camp ran from June 1940 to July 1941. It was re-opened in October 1941 to house mainly Italian internees until November 1944. It was one of the largest camps on the Island with space to grow vegetables, keep chickens and play football. It housed a large number of academics and artists and there were art exhibitions staged in the camp and a full programme of lectures and classes that internees could attend.

Sunflower bench

F. Summerhill Glen

OS Map ref. start: 389778
Terrain: Easy
Access: Drive out of Douglas on the main Onchan-Laxey road (A2), park outside the glen's upper entrance on Victoria Road (right at the mini-roundabout after the TT Grandstand). There is a bus stop near the entrance.

A woodland walk by the river, themed around fairies with many other curiosities and displays. It is floodlit at night (August-December) when it provides a different and enchanting experience from a day-time walk.

Summerhill Glen. Originally named 'Burnt Mill Hill', it was the site of the town's original reservoirs built in 1830s after a cholera outbreak. The glen was acquired by Douglas Borough Council and developed as a tourist attraction in 1932-1933: the work was carried out by 187 young men aged between 18 and 22 on a 'work for the workless' scheme. In recent years it has been populated by the Island's little people – the faeries!

Either side of the entrance are display cabinets of faeries and other Manx folklore. Immediately on the right is a tree trunk carved to represent a fairy throne. As one follows the tarmac path many trees are adorned with fairy doors. Continue forwards past a small left turning, soon one comes across a notice warning about the Moddey Dhoo – the

legendary big black dog whose main locus is Peel Castle. There are several lanterns that make good use of recycled plastic drink bottles: on the right is an area where seasonal and mythical images are projected at night.

Continue down the steps and turn right across the bridge with the river now on the left. Proceed up a flight of steps to a small open grassed area with two cannons that point out across Douglas Bay. In the shelter there are information boards about the glen. The steps on the right at the far side lead down to the lower entrance, turn left past the wood carving to return up the glen.

After a flight of steps take the path on the right, this is the high level route which allows one to look down on the river. Continue on past the turning on the left, the path drops down and crosses the river where one turns right to return to the upper entrance.

Summerhill Glen

G. Glen Falcon

OS Map ref. start: 380766
Terrain: Easy
Access: It is located on Broadway just off Douglas Promenade and behind the Villa Marina. There is on-street parking nearby. Bus services run along the Prom.

A small park with a stream running through it in a residential area.

Glen Falcon House. This glen was created out of the walled garden of Glen Falcon House, the small estate was built by William Okell who operated the Falcon Brewery from 1850s.

The brewery was opposite the upper entrance and the water from the stream that ran through his garden was used for brewing Okell's beers. After his death his widow donated the garden to the town of Douglas.

The upper entrance is opposite an apartment block that was formerly the Falcon Brewery. To the left of the grassed area is a path leading down some steps to the lower level and one is soon at the lower entrance on Broadway. Note the Glen Falcon plaque built into the wall. Take a sharp right up a flight of steps to return to the upper level grassed area.

H. Athol Park Glen

OS Map ref. start: 195689
Terrain: Easy
Access: Take the main road (A32) into Port Erin, turn left after the station and take the first left turning (before the road down to the bay). There is on-street parking near Athol Park Glen. Port Erin is served by buses and Steam Railway.

A small town-park laid out either side of a stream, it is popular with residents as it leads to a children's playground.

The main entrance is signed Athol Park Glen where a downslope takes one into the small glen itself. It is a grassed area with a small stream running down the middle with concreted paths either side and slab bridges crossing the waterway. It is easy enough to find one's own way round in under ten minutes.

Fairy house

Entrance to Athol Park Glen

Tree trunks have been adorned with fairy drawings and house doors. The left path passes brightly coloured benches and leads up to the children's play area, and beyond that the Steam Railway station. Proceed over the grass to cross the slab bridge to return to the entrance on the other side of the stream.